For Ed Brobout
with warm regards

Harry Levenson
9/19/66

I just figured the title
fit you. See if you get
anything out of it. It could
help. Happy Mother's Day 5-14-95
Bryan

P.S.— Read the Flaps. He-He-He.

Emotional
Health *IN THE*
WORLD OF WORK

**EXECUTIVE POLICY
AND LEADERSHIP** Series

Howard W. Johnson, Editor

Emotional Health *IN THE WORLD OF WORK*

———————————— Harry Levinson

HARPER & ROW, PUBLISHERS

NEW YORK, EVANSTON, AND LONDON

TO *Bobbie,*
Marc,
Kathy,
Anne,
and Brian

Contents

Preface

THIS BOOK IS A GUIDE FOR THE EVERYDAY USE OF EXECUTIVES. IT discusses how to begin to understand people, and how to apply that understanding to help those people in a business organization who act in ways which do not meet the demands of reality. It is directed to administrators and to occupational physicians—those people who have some responsibility for the work and work environment of others—because I have worked with them closely during the past ten years, and I write this in response to their needs. I hope that it will serve administrators directly by increasing their understanding of motivation and thereby prepare them better to help the people who are responsible to them. I hope also that they will find my suggestions for dealing with emotional stress constructive. I direct this to occupational physicians as a medium for their teaching in management education programs.

I conceive of emotional first aid as including not only what a person might do to help another who is upset or disturbed, but also what he might anticipate that could be stressful. In a limited sense, then, it includes prevention of emotional distress.

In order to help a person who is distressed, or to alleviate the pressures of stress situations, the reader will need to know how the personality functions. The first section of this book discusses some aspects of Freudian psychoanalytic theory. In my judgment, this theory offers the most comprehensive explanation of the forces that comprise and affect personality.

The reader will also need to know how to recognize personality malfunction, for that is often the result of emotional distress, and what to do about it. In the second section, the discussion centers around the more common kinds of reaction to stress and the meaning of those signs of malfunctioning that clinicians call symptoms. In this place of the study, there are specific suggestions about how to help another person whose stress is reflected in a certain kind of behavior.

Situational stresses on the job or related to the job, which can precipitate emotional disturbances, are the subject of the third section. Not all these stresses are avoidable. Like most events that come our way, if we are ready for them, we can usually take them in stride. If we can help another person be ready for them, or take specific steps to meet them, he, too, might be more likely to take them in stride.

In the fourth section are spelled out the principles of emotional first aid, the techniques derived from them, and the sources of professional help.

If our understanding of personality and psychological stress enables us to help individual people, perhaps the same understanding could give us a useful point of view from which to examine some of the policies and practices of management. In the fifth section we look at some widespread management practices with a view toward how they might be made even more effective and thereby more helpful to people.

This guide is a teaching device. It states some principles and tries to demonstrate ways in which the principles may be applied. It offers a constructive way of thinking about emotional stress and some suggested steps for helping with them.

HARRY LEVINSON

JANUARY 1964

Acknowledgments

I AM INDEBTED TO THE EDITORS OF THE *Harvard Business Review* for their permission to include in this volume, "What Killed Bob Lyons" (*Harvard Business Review*, 41:1, 127–144, January–February 1963), and "A Psychologist Looks at Executive Development" (*Harvard Business Review*, 40:5, 69–75, September–October 1962). The former has been adapted for Part I and the latter for Chapter 16. The editors of *Nation's Business* kindly permitted me to adapt "First Aid for Worried Workers" (*Nation's Business*, 48:9, 54–55 ff., September 1960) for Part IV, and "Cause and Cure of Personality Clashes" (*Nation's Business*, 49:4, 84–89, April 1961) for Chapter 17. "The Executive's Anxious Age," which appeared in *Think*, 28:7, 22–25, July–August 1962), has been adapted for part of Chapter 14 through the courtesy of the editors of that publication.

Drs. Joseph Satten and Roy W. Menninger made many important suggestions for the original version of "What Killed Bob Lyons." Professors Douglas McGregor, Edgar H. Schein, of the School of Industrial Management of MIT, and Professor Thomas M. Lodahl, of Cornell University did the same for "A Psychologist Looks at Executive Development." Drs. Satten, Menninger, and Harold J. Mandl, my colleagues at The Menninger Foundation, took time from their own very busy schedules to give me the benefit of their criticism of the manuscript. I am deeply grateful to them for their continuing interest and help. Of course I am alone responsible for what came of their comments.

Mrs. Helen Friend's creative editorial help is a part of each page and the conception of the whole. Mrs. Jean Senecal devoted many evenings and weekends to typing the manuscript.

To them, and to Drs. Karl and William C. Menninger, whose interest in mental health in industry made mine possible, I want to express my deepest appreciation.

H.L.

Emotional
Health *IN THE*
WORLD OF WORK

A Special Note to the Reader

THROUGHOUT THIS BOOK THERE ARE MANY CASE ILLUSTRATIONS. For some the reader will wish he had more information. None has the completeness of detail of a case history compiled by a clinician. These are not cases from clinical practice, but rather incidents from business life as they were recounted by business executives. They have been altered only to make certain they cannot be identified, and to correct grammar. Occasionally I have inserted an interpretation. They are real problems which executives had to face, as they saw them. The reader is also likely to see emotional problems in the same form, and to have to deal with them on the basis of such information.

PART I

WHAT KILLED BOB LYONS?

———————

THE FUNDAMENTAL TASK OF AN ADMINISTRATOR IS TO MAKE IT possible for an organization of people to accomplish the purposes for which they are associated. As he goes about his daily work, he spends most of his time working with people. He dictates correspondence to a secretary, holds a conference of his immediate staff, reviews the problems of the marketing department, considers forthcoming labor negotiations, and carries on a variety of other activities with people. In the process, he observes that a promising young middle management executive seems to have lost some of his zest. The marketing department, he notes, has been at odds for three weeks, unable to agree on a new program. The director of labor relations seems to be heavy-handed in his job, and no amount of advice has any effect on his behavior. The vice president of finance seems to think only of figures, and he is insensitive to the feelings of the other vice presidents. Sometimes the secretary comes to work with red-rimmed eyes and seems desperately to want to talk, yet hesitant to do so.

The executive has to do something about each of these problems if the work of the organization is to progress. But what? How does he understand what is happening? What really lies behind "poor communication," or "departmental conflict," or the

1

dramatic slump of a man who has unquestionable potential? And what can the executive, who is a not a psychologist or a psychiatrist, do?

Let us begin by recognizing that the human organism is complex. Like any complex system, whether mechanically constructed or biologically evolved, much that goes on "inside" is hidden from view. Unless we are to take the machine apart each time it does not function well, we must try to infer from its performance, even its sounds, what goes on internally and what can be done about its malfunction. The automobile mechanic, for example, needs only to hear the motor to know that the tappets are loose. To come to this conclusion, he needs to know how the motor is constructed, how it functions, and how to recognize those things that commonly go wrong with it.

We can understand the human personality only from the behavior we see, according to the theory we construct to explain that behavior. If our theory enables us to predict behavior, then we can assume that we understand what is going on inside that leads to the behavior. This section will discuss behavior and a theory that explains it. Our theory offers a way to understand the personality as if it were in fact made up of components. But when we discuss the parts of the personality we are referring only to theoretical ideas. The theory will also help us understand the sources of the personality's energy, and the way in the which the personality works to preserve and maintain itself.

Let us examine a difficult and painful problem, the case of Bob Lyons, to juxtapose behavior and theory.

CHAPTER 1

Why Did It Happen?

THOSE WHO KNEW BOB LYONS THOUGHT EXTREMELY WELL OF him. He was a highly successful executive who held an important postion in his company. As his superiors saw him, he was aggressive and adept in getting things done through other people. He worked hard and set a vigorous pace. He drove himself relentlessly. In less than ten years with his company, he had moved through several positions of responsibility.

Lyons had always been a good athlete. He was proud of his skill in swimming, hunting, golf, and tennis. In his college days he had won letters in football and baseball. On weekends he preferred to hunt, or to rebuild and repair projects around the house, interspersing sports for a change of pace. He was usually engaged, it seemed, in hard, physical work.

His life was not all work, however. He was active in his church and in the Boy Scouts. His wife delighted in entertaining and in being with other people, so their social life was a round of parties and social activities. They shared much of this life with their three children.

3

Early in the spring of his ninth year with his company, Bob Lyons spoke with the vice president to whom he reported. "Things are a little quiet around here," he said. "Most of the big projects are over. The new building is finished and we have a lot of things running smoothly which four years ago were all fouled up. I don't like this idea of just riding a desk and looking out the window. I like action."

About a month later, Lyons was assigned additional responsibilities. He rushed into them with his usual vigor. Once again he seemed to be buoyant and cheerful. After six months on the assignment, Lyons had the project rolling smoothly. Again he spoke to his vice president, reporting that he was out of projects. The vice-president, pleased with Lyons' performance, told him that he had earned the right to do a little dreaming and planning. Furthermore, dreaming and planning were a necessary part of the position he now held, toward which he had aspired for so long. Bob Lyons listened as the vice-president spoke, but it was plain to the latter that the answer did not satisfy him.

About three months after this meeting, the vice-president began to notice that replies to his memos and inquiries were not coming back from Lyons with their usual rapidity. He noticed also that Lyons was developing a tendency to put things off, a most unusual behavior pattern for him. He observed that Lyons became easily angered and disturbed over minor difficulties that previously had not irritated him at all.

Bob Lyons then became involved in a conflict with two other executives over a policy issue. Such conflicts were not unusual in the company, as inevitably there would be varying points of view on many issues. The conflict was not a personal one, but the vice-president did have to intervene before a solution could be reached. In the process of resolving the conflict, Lyons' point of view prevailed on some questions but not on others.

A few weeks after this conflict had been resolved, Lyons went to the vice-president's office. He wanted to have a long private talk, he said. His first words were, "I'm losing my grip. The old steam is gone. I've had diarrhea for four weeks and several times in the past three weeks I've lost my breakfast. I'm worried and yet I don't know what about. I feel that some people have lost confidence in me."

He talked with the vice-president for an hour and a half. The vice-president recounted his achievements in the company to reassure him. He then asked if Lyons thought he should see a doctor. Lyons agreed that he should, and in the presence of the vice-president, called his family doctor for an appointment.

By this time, the vice-president was very much concerned. He called Mrs. Lyons and arranged to meet her for lunch the next day. She reported that in addition to her husband's other symptoms, he had had difficulty sleeping. She was relieved that the vice-president had called because she was beginning to become worried and had herself planned to call the vice-president. Both were now alarmed. They decided that they should get Lyons into a hospital rather than wait for the doctor's appointment, which was still a week off.

The next day Lyons was taken to the hospital. Meanwhile, with Mrs. Lyons' permission, the vice-president reported to the family doctor about Lyons' recent job behavior and the nature of their conversations. When the vice-president had finished, the doctor concluded, "All he needs is a good rest. We don't want to tell him that it may be mental or nervous." The vice-president replied that he did not know what the cause was, but he knew that Bob Lyons needed help quickly.

Neither the president nor the vice-president knew why

Bob Lyons might have "needed a good rest." He had, in fact, complained that he had not been working hard enough. Obviously he was worried, and equally obviously he had distressing physical symptoms which seemed to be related to his worries. But why? Could it be that he had not been promoted fast enough? Was he disappointed in himself? Or had he been advanced too fast? Was he overwhelmed in his job? Having done so much, did he feel there was nothing challenging left for him to do? Was he dismayed because he realized he was no longer a young man? The two executives could only speculate.

During five days in the hospital, Lyons was subjected to extensive laboratory tests. The vice-president visited him daily. He seemed to welcome the rest and the sedation at night. He said he was eating and sleeping much better. He talked about company problems, but he did not speak freely without encouragement. While Lyons was out of the room, another executive who shared his hospital room confided to the vice-president that he was worried about Lyons. "He seems to be so morose and depressed, I'm afraid he's losing his mind," the executive said.

The vice-president had kept the president informed. By this time, the president was also becoming concerned. The president talked to a psychiatrist and planned to talk to Lyons about psychiatric treatment if his doctor did not suggest it. Meanwhile, Lyons was discharged from the hospital as being without physical illness, and his doctor recommended a vacation.

Lyons then remained at home for several days, where he was again visited by the vice-president. He and his wife took a trip to visit friends. He was then ready to come back to work, but the president suggested that he take another week off. The president also suggested that he and Lyons visit together when Lyons returned.

On the day Lyons returned from his out-of-town visit, the president telephoned him at home. Mrs. Lyons could not find him to answer the telephone. An hour later she still had not found him, and in her concern she called the vice-president. By the time the vice-president arrived at the Lyons' home, the police were already there. Bob Lyons had shot himself.

This story is not an unusual one. But probably no other single consequence of an emotional problem is as disturbing to those who must live with it as is suicide. No doubt Bob Lyons' colleagues suffered almost as much anguish as his family did. The president and the vice-president were concerned long afterward. They wondered if, despite their conscientious efforts, they had in some way been at fault or if they could have prevented this suicide. Neither his family nor his colleagues could understand why it happened. It made no sense to them that a succesful man in the prime of his life, like Lyons, should destroy himself.

Lyons' reaction to his emotional problem may have been extreme, but other severe reactions to similar emotional problems are not rare in the work place. Executives, managers, supervisors, occupational physicians, and to a lesser extent, all employees, frequently must cope on the job with the emotional distress of others. For those who have to cope with the behavior, such distress is a problem. The behavior of those who are distressed is an attempt to solve underlying problems, as we shall see later. Many reactions are of lesser proportion than Lyons', but all have four factors in common:

1. They are painful for both the person who suffers from them and those who must deal with him.

2. They are usually destructive to both the sufferer and the organization.

3. The origins of the reaction are almost always more complex than most people realize, and only infrequently are even the precipitating events clear.

4. Rarely does the person responsible for dealing with on-the-job behavior know what he should do about it.

As a result, few businesses have ways of dealing with these problems even reasonably well and management actions tend to range from abrupt firing to hostile discipline to procrastination, which in some instances goes on for years. Often there is a vacillating series of management efforts to cope with the problem, accompanied by feelings of guilt, failure, and anger on the part of those who must make the managerial decisions. Emotional problems, then, are contagious. The disturbance suffered by one person has its effects on the emotions of others.

How can we understand what happened to Bob Lyons and in what ways his problem relates to other problems with which an executive must deal? The customary common-sense reasons do not really explain. He had no serious illness. He did not fail in his business activity. There was no indication of difficulty in his family life. In the story told by the vice-president, the pattern of development is too obvious to attribute Bob Lyons' death to an accident or to chance.

WAS IT HEREDITARY?

Can we say Bob Lyons inherited a tendency to suicide? Man inherits certain capacities and traits, but these are essentially physiological. He inherits the color of his eyes, the size of his nose, and other physical features. He inherits certain sensory and motor capacities; that is, he will be able to see, hear, or feel physical stimuli—color, sound, warmth—

more or less keenly. Newborn infants in a hospital nursery will vary widely in their response to such stimuli. Some are calm and placid; someone could drop a metal tray with considerable clatter, but these children would continue to sleep. Others, however, would be startled and awaken crying.

The infants are not simply "born that way" because they inherited genes leading to calmness or restlessness from their parents. There is evidence to indicate that the pre-birth environment has much to do with how the infant behaves.[1]*

Among human beings, certainly the mother's diet, the illnesses she has during pregnancy, and her general physical condition have their effects on the infant. Hereditary influences on specific behavorial acts are extremely difficult to demonstrate.

SOMETHING PHYSICAL?

Apparently man also inherits a capacity to coordinate his muscles with greater or lesser efficiency. If a person inherits excellent coordination potential and develops it, he may ultimately become a good athlete or a good musician. If he inherits a better than usual capacity for abstracting sights and sounds, he may have the makings of an artist. Man does not inherit athletic or artistic skill, but some men and women inherit such a high level of sensitivity and physiological harmony that they seem to have a "natural bent" for certain activities.

Some apparently are born with greater general intelligence. They may therefore have the potential for dealing

---

* Superscripts refer to the References at the end of this volume.

with their environments with better reasoning power and more effective judgment. Others have more specialized capacities: the ability to abstract ideas readily, a good memory, and so on. Differences in level of awareness, which appear in some instances at birth, make for different kinds of interactions with the environment. The irritable infant will have a quite different relationship with his mother than will the placid child. The child who walks and talks early comes into contact earlier with a wider range of experiences than does another child from the same general environment, whose skills may develop later.

Heredity, then, to a large extent determines a person's potential development, in the sense that everyone has to be short or tall, intelligent or unintelligent, and have different thresholds of his various senses. Each person is different in the combination of endowments he has and in the degree to which they enable him to cope with life's stresses.

While hereditary factors influence man's behavior in gross or general ways, they have little direct effect on his specific behavior. Because of the high level of development of the frontal lobes of his brain, man is capable of both abstract and reflective thinking. He is also capable of a wide range of emotions. These capacities for thought and feeling make man extremely responsive to many nuances of environmental stimulation. They also make it possible for him to initiate a wide range of actions in keeping with his thoughts and feelings, as well as in response to his environment, particularly to the other people in it.

FAMILY INFLUENCE?

Another environmental factor that has an important influence on behavior is the extremely long period, particularly in Western cultures, during which the human child is dependent upon his parents. The intimacy of these relationships and the many social pressures transmitted through the parents to the children make family influences extremely important in guiding and controlling behavior. The extended period of dependency also presents a psychological problem because each person must then resolve the conflict between his wish for the pleasures of dependency and his desire to have the gratification of being an independent adult. No one ever completely gives up the former or completely obtains the latter.

Each seeks some way of being interdependent with others so that he can depend on them without losing his pride—because they in turn depend on him. Everyone, as indicated above, has conflicting wishes about his dependency needs. The way in which each person resolves this conflict leads to certain kinds of behavior. Some who have not resolved the conflict well will always be more dependent than others. To depend heavily on other people becomes a mode of life for them. Some who have resolved this conflict reasonably well can assume a dependent role when necessary, but can easily remain independent under other circumstances. Some have rejected or denied such needs and will avoid situations in which they might have to depend on others.

So, too, different companies will require different degrees of dependency in their employees. And people tend to seek employment in companies that meet their particular dependency needs. People who remain in a stable public utility company for a long time will be more dependent on the company for their security than will itinerant salesmen who sell magazines on commission. The fact that such a range of possibilities is available at work for fulfilling these needs is one of the health-giving aspects of work in business organizations.

Therefore we cannot very well say that Bob Lyons committed suicide because of heredity. Perhaps hereditary factors interacting with environmental factors led to his death, but in our present state of knowledge it would be extremely difficult to demonstrate a hereditary predisposition which contributed to his self-destruction. We must turn to more purely psychological factors for an explanation.

CHAPTER 2

Something on the Inside

EXECUTIVES FREQUENTLY DESPAIR OVER EXPLAINING WHY someone like Bob Lyons would kill himself. They say, "There must have been something odd inside of him that drove him into doing it." In a way, they are partially right. Inside all of us are many emotional drives which seem odd when we do not understand them.

For an approach toward understanding, return for a moment to the first paragraph of the description of Lyons. Look at these phrases in that paragraph: "highly successful," "aggressive," "adept in getting things done through other people," "worked hard," "set a vigorous pace," and "drove himself relentlessly." These phrases speak of drive or energy. The subsequent two paragraphs describe other ways in which he discharged his energy. Some of these ways were highly useful to himself, his company, his family, and his friends. Others had a destructive potential: "He drove himself relentlessly." In fact, his difficulties seemed to begin when his job no longer provided opportunities to drive himself at his work.

THE DUAL DRIVE THEORY

```
CONSTRUCTIVE DRIVE
                                        PSYCHOLOGICAL ENERGY
DESTRUCTIVE DRIVE
```

The theories of Sigmund Freud aid in understanding the importance of such drives. Freud said that there were two constantly operating psychological drives in the personality: a *constructive drive* and a *destructive drive.* Just as there are always processes of growth and destruction in all biological matter, anabolism and catabolism, so there are similar processes in the personality. These drives constitute the basic, primitive energy sources for the personality. The constructive drive (sometimes referred to as the *libido*) is the source of feelings of love, creativity, and psychological growth. The destructive drive gives rise to feelings of anger and hostility. The twin forces are variously referred to as love and hate; in terms of Greek mythology, as Eros and Thanatos, or sex and aggression. (When used in this way, both terms have a far broader meaning than they do in ordinary usage.)

A major psychological task for every human being is to fuse these drives in such a way that the constructive drive tempers, guides, and controls the destructive drive, so that the energy from both sources may be used in a man's own self-interest and that of society. If the destructive drive is described as the aggressive drive (recognizing that we are using the word *aggressive* according to its dictionary meaning and not as synonymous with assertion, as in ordinary usage), it is certainly far better for a person to use his aggressive drive, tempered by larger amounts of the constructive drive, in the pursuit of a career, the creation of a family, and in business competition than in socially forbidden destruction, as might be the case if the drives were not adequately fused. In short, there are many socially acceptable ways for using aggressive drive, such as combating ignorance, vanquishing the enemy in wartime, or entertaining the public in competitive sports.

Bob Lyons devoted much energy to his work, his family, and his community. He was successful in his work. He apparently enjoyed his family, and he helped make his community a better place to live. From these behaviors it appears that much of his constructive and aggressive energy, and more of the former than the latter, was well fused and channeled. In some ways, however, his constructive drive was less dominant, for he drove himself relentlessly.

PERSONALITY STRUCTURE: THE ID

The two drives are included in a part of the personality (a set of functions, not a physical entity) to which Freud gave the name *id*, the Latin word for "it." In addition to the two basic drives, the id also includes many of the memories and experiences that a person can no longer recall.

The brain acts as a vast tape recorder. It records our various experiences more or less clearly, depending on the intensity of the experiences and how we interpreted them when they occurred. Theoretically, a person should be able to recall all experiences, and feelings about those experiences, he has had. Under hypnosis, in psychoanalysis, and under the influence of some drugs, a person can recall many of them, even though he could not do so before, no matter how hard he tried. Many of these memories, feelings, and impulses (impulses are derivatives of drives) are "buried" in the id, but they are still "alive" and they would be expressed if there were not adequate controls. Here is how that "bury-ing" process may have worked in Bob Lyons' case:

To judge from his behavior, he may have learned in child-hood that the only way to obtain parental love was by good performance. If high performance was the price of love, Lyons may well have resented his parents' attitude. But since such a conscious feeling of anger toward his parents would have been painful to live with, it was "buried." Lyons was no longer aware of his anger toward them, but it re-mained with him. The id has no sense of time; it is inconsist-ent, contradictory, and without special techniques, it is not accessible to logic or persuasion. Thus the early experiences that caused Bob Lyons' feelings of resentment were still "alive" and painful in the id part of the personality.

In discussing the drives, we have said that psychological growth and survival require more of the constructive drive, implying that there are differences in the amount of drive energy. We assume that there are differences among people in how much drive energy they have. It is not known how these differences come about, nor is there any satisfactory way of specifying amount other than grossly and compara-tively.

PERSONALITY STRUCTURE: THE SUPER EGO

Not only did Bob Lyons have the major psychological task of balancing or fusing his constructive and aggressive drives, but he also had to discharge these drives in socially accept-able ways. It might have been permissible in more primitive times to hit a man on the head and take his wife, but today there are stringent cultural controls on how love and aggres-sion may be expressed.

These controls on the expression of our basic drives vary

from culture to culture, even from one social class to another; but they are transmitted through the parents and other authority figures to children. Early in the child's development, the parents control and direct him. They permit some forms of behavior, but prohibit others. As the child grows older, he incorporates into his own personality what his parents have taught him. He will incorporate these rules and values most effectively if he feels an affectionate bond with the parents and wants to be like them. This is one of the reasons the parent-child relationship is so important and why it should enable the child to feel happy and secure.

Various values and rules can be "pounded into" the child, but these tend not to be genuinely his. He lives by them only as long as external pressures require him to, and he abandons them later. Some parents who try to force piety and goodness into their children are dismayed to find them neither pious nor good when they grow up.

When the child develops a conscience, he becomes self-governing. In Freudian terms, he has developed a *superego*. The superego is made up of four parts: (1) the values of the culture as transmitted through the parents, teachers, friends, ministers, and so on (religion, ethics); (2) rules, prohibitions, and taboos; (3) an ego ideal—that image of ourselves at our future best which we never fully attain and which causes us to be perennially discontented with ourselves; and (4) a police-judging or self-critical function.*

The superego begins to develop in the child when the words "no" or "don't" enter his world. Its general form tends

---

* Some theorists separate the superego and the conscience. They limit the superego to the values and the ego ideal (parts 1 and 3 above) and refer to the rules (part 2) and the self-critical function (part 4) as the conscience. While that distinction is important to theorists, for our purposes we can ignore it. We shall consider the conscience to be a part of the superego and to include all four factors in the superego, as above.

to be established by the time the child enters elementary school, although it becomes further refined and expanded as a person grows up. Some features of the superego, developed early in life, are not conscious. The person is no longer aware of why he must live by certain rules and values; he knows only that if he does not do so, he feels uncomfortable. Some children, for example, feel that they must be the best students in their class. They may not know why they have this feeling, but if they are not always successful, they feel they are no good.

CONSCIENCE AND CULTURE

Because the superego is acquired from the culture in which a person lives (principally through the medium of his parents and later by incorporating the values, rules, and ideals of others he respects), it is reinforced by the culture. A man's superego may keep him from stealing, for example, but there are also social penalties for stealing.

Among the directions that the superego controls are those concerning the direction of the constructive and aggressive drives, the ways in which a person may love and may hate, and what kind of an adult person he should be. A man may not, in Western cultures, love another woman as he loves his wife. He may express affection to other men in Italy and Spain by embracing them, but not in the United States. He may express his anger verbally, but not in physical attack. He may direct some of his aggressive drive in areas of work, sports, and community activities that are not commonly regarded as feminine.

There are many ingredients among families and subcultures which become part of the superegos of people in those groups. Among middle-class American families there is a heavy emphasis on achievement, cleanliness, good manners, hard work, and on the avoidance of open expressions of hostility. Lower-class families, particularly those at lowest socio-economic levels, are not particularly concerned about these values. Some fundamentalist religious groups prohibit drinking and dancing. Some groups teach their children that they are sinful by nature. Others permit a much wider range of behavior.

The heavy influence of the parents on the shaping of personality makes it possible for certain styles of behavior to be transmitted from father to son to grandson. Much behavior that people tend to regard as hereditary because it seems to "run in families" is actually due to environmental influences.

"KNOW THEN THYSELF"

A man's opinion of himself, or his self-image, is related to the superego. One measure of self-evaluation is the disparity between the ego ideal and how he regards himself at present. When he is depreciated by people who are important to him, this reinforces the critical aspects of the superego and lowers self-esteem. When, however, self-esteem is enhanced, it counteracts the criticism of the superego and neutralizes some of the aggressive drive, thus stimulating the person to an expanded, more confident view and use of himself and his capacities.

It has been said that no wound is as painful as that inflicted by the superego. When a person behaves in ways that contradict the values and rules he has made a part of himself, or when in his judgment he feels he is falling short of his ego ideal, the superego induces a feeling of guilt. For most people, guilt feelings are so strong and so painful that they try to make up for violations of the superego by some form of atonement. One form of atonement is self-punishment. The religious concept of penance is a recognition of this phenomenon. Restitution is another way of relieving guilt feelings. It is not unusual to see newspaper articles about people who have anonymously sent money to the government because they cheated on their taxes years before. Government officials speak of this as "conscience money."

Because the development of the superego begins early, it is easy for the child to learn to judge himself more harshly than he should. With his limited capacity to reason, he may hold himself to blame for events that he had nothing to do with. For example, suppose a two-year-old child is severely hurt in a fall. His four-year-old brother, who must inevitably have some feelings of hostility and rivalry toward the younger child, may come to feel that he is responsible for the fall. As a matter of fact, he had nothing to do with it, but for the small child, a wish is often tantamount to the act. To wish the younger child to be destroyed may be the same to a four-year-old as actually having pushed him. He may then harbor irrational guilt feelings for many years thereafter, completely unaware that he has such feelings or how they came about.

Since there is love and hate in every relationship, children have considerable hostility toward their parents. Usually, young children do not understand that their hostile feelings are not "bad" and that parents will not be destroyed because they have such feelings. As a result, most of us carry a considerable load of irrational guilt feelings. One of the major tasks in some forms of psychological treatment is to make conscious the sources of irrational unconscious feelings. When a person recognizes the sources of his feelings and has worked out more effective ways of dealing with them, these irrational feelings will no longer be such a problem.

THE GOVERNOR

The superego, then, becomes a built-in governor. A well-developed superego provides a person with an automatic, consistent, continuous guide to behavior. He knows what he believes, what he should do in various situations, what he should be working toward, and how adequately his behavior meets his standards.

Without a superego, a person would have no internal guide to behavior. He would merely give vent to his impulses as they arose. Some people, for example, who do not adequately control their behavior and are sent to prison, are model prisoners. When they are discharged, however, they promptly get into trouble again.

As an automatic protective device, the superego often operates in a subtle fashion. It shuts out some thoughts and ideas so that they never trouble a person. For most of us, the question, "Should I or should I not steal?", never arises.

When it is a consistent guide to behavior, the superego makes it possible for people to behave in a predictable way. We know what they will say and do under different circumstances. We therefore feel we can depend on them. But some people behave one way one time and another way another time, even when the circumstances appear to be the same. Without intensive study of all the forces at play at any given time, we cannot know whether they will fulfill their responsibilities at any given time. As a result, we judge them to be inconsistent and therefore undependable. Their superegos do not serve effectively to counteract other pressures.

If the rules and values taught to the child are inconsistent, then his superego will be inconsistent, and his behavior will appear to be inconsistent. If the parent teaches the child not to steal and then operates his business dishonestly, the child may well be honest in some things but not in others.

Some children are taught many, many rules of behavior, and these are strictly enforced by the parents. For such children, the behavioral paths are straight and narrow. Almost anything they do is wrong. For them, the superego becomes a harsh taskmaster. It continues the tight controls the parents initiated. It severely limits the way a person can behave; it forbids many activities as being too frivolous or childish or the like. We speak of such people as being "strait laced." If there are too many too strict rules, then life is not much fun —the person feels that he must always be "good." Even having fun may be "bad." When he is not "good" by his own high standards, then he is burdened excessively with feelings of guilt. The superego demands that he atone for his "bad" behavior.

When a person feels that he *must* do something, there is a quality of compulsion in his behavior. The feeling of *must* comes from the guilt feelings engendered by the superego. The person drives himself when he feels he has to atone for a violation of his superego, but most of the time, he is not aware of the guilt feelings. He knows only that if he does not drive himself on, he will feel restless and uncomfortable.

People who live with tyrannical superegos have the feeling that there is so much they *ought* to do or *must* do, as contrasted with the feeling that there is so much they would enjoy doing. Unless they are constantly doing what they feel they ought to do, then they feel uneasy. Bob Lyons, for example, not only drove himself relentlessly, but also usually had to be working hard.

HOME AND JOB

Not everything we do, of course, is completely influenced by our emotional drives. Environment plays a part and should be considered in the attempt to understand Bob Lyons' suicide. For, in addition to the task of balancing or fusing the two drives in keeping with the strictures of the superego, a person must deal with his external environment. At times, this environment is the source of affection, support, and security. The child in his mother's arms, a man enjoying himself among his friends, a woman in a happy marriage, a man building a business, a minister serving his congregation, all draw emotional nourishment from the environment. Such nourishment strengthens the constructive forces of the personality.

When looked at closely, *needs for status and esteem are essentially needs for love and affection.* Few can survive long without giving and receiving love, though often in ways that are thoroughly disguised, even from the self. Status needs have to do with the constructive forces of the personality. When a man seeks symbols of status, he simply searches for some concrete indication that some others hold him in esteem. To speak of status needs is to say that the person needs infusions of affection and gratification to foster his own strength.

However, the environment may also stimulate aggression: anger and jealousy, exploitation, competition for various advantages, economic reverses, wars, and so on. Every person has to deal with the realities of his environment—whether with the necessities of earning a living, the frustration of an unsolved problem, the achievement of personal goals, or the development of satisfying relationships with other people. Lyons was actively involved with all these things in his environment.

CHAPTER 3

Ego and Reality

_____

THE ID DRIVES, THE SUPEREGO, AND THE ENVIRONMENT MUST be kept in close enough balance so that the personality will not be disrupted. For if it is disrupted, the result is mental illness.

Some mechanism is required to do the balancing, to serve as the executive part of the personality. Such a component of personality must fuse the drives, control their discharge in keeping with the conditions set by the superego, and act upon the environment. Freud gave the name *ego* to this set of functions. We tend to speak of the ego as a thing; actually the term is merely a short way of describing the many different ways through which the personality controls its more primitive impulses and deals with what goes on outside itself.

The ego includes a wide range of mental activities: The ability to *recall*, for example, makes it possible to remember from one experience to the next and thereby to learn. *Perception* is that complex activity by which we see, hear, feel, taste, smell, and combine all these senses into an understanding of what goes on around us and within us. If, for example, we could not feel pain or see danger, we could not protect ourselves from internal or external threats. When we give our attention to some event, we *concentrate* on it. We select it from among many other events.

We are able to select from a myriad of impressions those that go together in some fashion. For example, from the many impressions of light and dark that strike your eye at this moment, you attend to the dark impressions, abstracting them from the white background. You perceive their shapes, relate these to previous experiences, which you now recall, and you read the dark impressions as letters combined into words. You combine the words into *concepts*—thoughts, ideas, interpretations. All these activities are ego functions. They enable you to receive, organize, interpret, and act on stimuli.

The ego develops, except in those who suffer retardation or severe illness, as the person grows. How much his effectiveness increases, and in what directions, depends on many different factors, but mainly on the experiences he has been and is being exposed to. The ego acquires and stores information in the form of memory images, particularly information and experiences that previously led to the successful solution of problems. These images are not merely stored; they are integrated so that they can be called upon to help us solve problems we face every day.

For example, in the case of Bob Lyons, the vice-president quickly got in touch with Mrs. Lyons and together they quickly had Lyons admitted to a hospital. The vice-president was calling upon all that he had learned about behavior in his own experience, together with what he had read. By putting together what he perceived, how he organized his perceptions, the abstractions he made from these perceptions and the judgments he made about them, and recalling previous knowledge about similar experiences, he came to a decision. He knew what to do because, either in thought or action, he had been along this path before. He could *imagine* both what he should do and what might happen if he did not do it.

A similar thing would happen if the problem were an internal one. When an impulse arises from one of the drives, in effect the ego contains the impulse until it has checked with the superego and until it has determined what the consequences of acting on the impulse will be. Suppose a valued customer writes you a letter complaining about the poor quality of one of your products. As you read the letter, you note from his description that he has been misusing the product and blaming you. Your initial impulse is to write him an angry letter in return, telling him what a fool he is. But the superego will not tolerate your hurting his feelings, and the ego, anticipating what might happen, concludes that it will cost too much to criticize a customer this way. Instead, you write him, offering to make good on the product and tactfully suggesting ways to avoid further difficulty with it.

In this case, the ego presumably checked its memory images to find the best way available for handling the impulse. It found an effective method. What started to be a direct, aggressive attack was then contained, diminished, refined, and expressed in modified fashion to meet both the conditions of the superego and the demands of the environment. In the tactful suggestion, the aggression is tempered and fused so that it becomes constructive criticism.

The ability to control id impulses well by checking memory images, refining the impulses and fusing them for discharge, indicates a strong ego or psychological maturity. Inability to do so adequately indicates that the person does not have adequate ego strength or that he is immature. The ego acts on the basis of what is called the reality principle: *"What are the long-run consequences of this behavior?"*

The process of checking the memory images and organizing a response is called "thinking." Thinking is trial action or a "dry run." Sometimes it goes on consciously, but much of the time it is an unconscious process. Thinking serves to delay impulses until they can be discharged in the most satisfactory way the person knows. When a person acts impulsively in minor ways (for instance, being inconsiderate of another person), such behavior is called "thoughtless."

A store manager may be said to have poor judgment if he buys items without thinking through their marketing possibilities, or merely because he likes the salesman who sold them. This is another form of impulsiveness or immaturity. Marketing experts count on the irrational impulsiveness of the public when they create in supermarkets such a vast array of stimuli that the ego does not function as well as it might. Impulse-buying will result unless the ego is bolstered by additional support in the form of a shopping list and a budget.

The ego is constantly concerned with the cost and consequences of any action. In other words, the ego is concerned with psychological economy.

BELEAGUERED EGO

The ego is always under psychological pressure. To carry on its integrating function well requires considerable strength. *Strength comes from several sources: the basic inherited capacities; experiences of love and gratification, which enhance the constructive forces; the development of skills and abilities, which help it master the environment; and the physical health of the person.* The ego may be weakened through physical injury or illness—a brain tumor, a debilitating sickness—or by having to devote too much of its energy to repressing or otherwise coping with severe multiple or chronic emotional pressures.

The ego cannot deal with all the stimuli that impinge upon it. It is constantly being bombarded with all kinds of data. It cannot deal with all the information it has in the form of past experiences and present ones. It must be selective. Some data are therefore passed directly on to the id. The ego is never consciously aware of them. Furthermore, it is not able to resolve all its psychological problems, some of which are extremely painful. These problems are repressed, or pushed down into the id.

Here is a more personal example. Young children lead extremely active lives. They have many pleasant moments and some painful ones. They remember experiences from day to day and recall exciting events, like a trip to the zoo, with great relish. Now try to remember your own early childhood experiences, especially those that occurred before the ages of four or five. Probably you will be able to recall few in any detail, if you can recall any at all. Many other experiences of childhood, adolescence, and even adulthood are beyond voluntary recall. Yet, under hypnosis they can be recalled. This information, perhaps much of it not immediately necessary to solve today's problems, is stored in the id.

Memory traces of some experiences, which might help solve problems, are stored in the ego, though even they are usually not conscious. You may be surprised to find yourself at home, having driven from work while preoccupied with a problem without even having noticed the turns, stop lights, or other cars. Obviously, you used many cues and did many specific things to get home safely, though you did so without being aware of what you were doing.

A final example illustrates the way the ego deals with impulses from the id. Suppose an attractive secretary comes to work in a new dress whose lines are calculated to stimulate the interest of men—in short, to stimulate the sexual impulse. When this impulse reaches the ego of one of the men in the office, acting within the limits set by the superego ("Look but don't touch!") and its judgment of the consequences of giving vent to the impulse, ("You'll destroy your reputation!"), the ego will control and refine the impulse. He may then comment, "That's a pretty dress," a highly attentuated derivative of the original impulse. Another man with a more rigid superego might not notice the dress. His superego would protect him by automatically prohibiting the ego from being sensitive to such a stimulus.

ANXIETY AND DEFENSE

As we have said, the ego has two jobs. First, it has a balancing task. From the id come the constructive and destructive drives and the repressed memories. From the superego come the push-pull forces of "you must" and "you shall not," plus painful feelings of guilt. From the outside come all kinds of stimuli and pressures. The ego has to balance all these forces in such a manner that id impulses may be expressed in ways that do not produce guilt or bring punishment from the environment. Restriction of sexual life to marriage by middle-class American culture is an example of such an attempt at a solution. Or the ego may have to satisfy the superego while permitting modified discharge of id impulses in keeping with environmental demands. Achieving success in the business world is an example. Or the ego may have to meet the demands of the environment while not violating the superego and keeping id impulses well in hand. Trying to maintain good quality of production (a superego pressure) in the face of demand for increased quantity and the breakdown of a machine (both stimulating anger) is a case in point.

The second task of the ego is to synchronize these many forces into a system that works relatively smoothly, for the personality operates as a whole system all the time. In a sense, the ego is like the conductor of an orchestra. It is a creative, synthesizing part of the personality. It makes something unique out of the raw material of the id, the superego, the environment, and its own resources.

To do its balancing and synchronizing work, the ego requires two kinds of devices:

1. It needs *anxiety* to serve as an alarm system that alerts it to possible dangers to the personality's equilibrium. Anxiety itself is a symptom that something is wrong, just like fever.

2. It must have *defense mechanisms*, which are triggered by the alarm system and called into play. These will help it either to fend off the possible threats or counteract them. Anxiety can in fact cause such mechanisms to be brought into play without our ever being aware of it.

We are conscious of one aspect of anxiety whenever we are afraid of something. We have a feeling of unease or tension. For the most part, however, anxiety is much more subtle and complex. It operates spontaneously and unconsciously whenever the ego is threatened. Being unaware of its operation, we may not know consciously why we are restless, tense, or upset. Bob Lyons was worried, but he did not know why.

Everyone has experienced this anxiety. A feeling of tension and restlessness picked up by one person from another is very common. Apparently emotional disturbances can be "contagious" or are transferable. Sensing that the other person is upset makes one feel uneasy for reasons that are not very clear. One does not consciously decide that he is threatened, but he feels that he "can't relax," that he must be on guard.

There is no state of placid emotional stability, just as there is never a smooth ocean or an atmosphere devoid of air currents. Everyone is always engaged in maintaining his psychological equilibrium. Even when a person is asleep, his dreaming is an effort to resolve psychological problems, to discharge tension, and to maintain sleep. The workings of unconscious anxiety may be seen in a number of different ways.

Because anxiety is often unconscious, we must judge from thoughts, feelings, and behavior that the person is anxious. A man who is not getting his work done, though ordinarily he would, is not behaving normally. He may know only that he cannot concentrate as well as he usually does or that he is making too many errors. If we were to watch him closely and listen to his conversation, we might learn that he had recently heard about the probable introduction to his job of automated equipment. Though he seems on the surface to be untroubled about what he has heard, his behavior betrays his underlying concern.

Suppose you are driving your car down the street and a child dashes out from between parked cars into your path. You immediately slam on the brakes. For a moment you do not know whether you have hit the child. When you get out of the car, you see that you have not, but you find yourself shaking, your heart beating rapidly, your skin perspiring. You did not consciously cause any of these things to happen. The threat to your equilibrium, constituting a stress, aroused anxiety, which in turn mobilized the organism's resources for dealing with the emergency. A similar experience is commonplace among athletes. Some of them experience such psychological tension before competitive events that they cannot eat; if they do, they throw up.

Here we are speaking of conscious anxiety. We are aware of certain threats and react to them. But at another, unconscious level, our reaction is disproportionate to the event. There is no objective reason for the driver to continue to be anxious when he discovers that he has not hit the child. The overt threat has passed. Yet he has come so close to violating his superego prohibitions against hurting another person that he may continue to shake for hours and may even dream about the event to the point of having nightmares.

It is understandable why the athlete would want to win the game for conscious reasons. Why the competition should cause him such violent physical reaction is a more complex problem. He himself does not know why his whole physiological and psychological organism gets itself so geared up that he cannot tolerate food. He is unaware that he is selectively mobilizing his forces to deal with the emergency. Determined to win the game, trying to live up to the standards of his superego, and seeking to earn the accolades of his coach and fans, the athlete mobilizes all his energies for the competition. His body cannot "take time" or spare the body fluids to digest food. In order to maintain an equilibrium under these conditions of stress, the body rejects the food. Because the reaction to a game is so extreme, unconscious anxiety must be at work.

EGO DEFENSES

In order to penetrate deeply enough into Bob Lyons' reasons for suicide, we must go beyond assuming that he was anxious and under stress. We need to see why his ego was not able to keep from destroying itself—why the ego's defense mechanisms did not enable him to cope with his anxiety.

There are a number of personality mechanisms that operate automatically to help the ego maintain or regain its equilibrium. These mechanisms may be viewed as falling into three broad classes:

1. One group has to do with shaping or forming the personality. These mechanisms are required for growth. Included in this category is *identification*, the process of behaving like someone else. A man identifies himself with his boss when he dresses or speaks as his boss does. Women identify with a leading movie star when they adopt her hair style. Identification may often be temporary. A person can identify with someone else and change his behavior. Another device, *introjection*, is a stronger form of identification, although the line between them is hazy. When one introjects the mannerisms or attitudes of another, he makes these firmly a part of himself. They are permanent. Some people introject the values of their parents and thereby become like them.

2. Another group of mechanisms are universally used devices which are required to control, guide, refine, and channel the basic drives or impulses from the id. These mechanisms operate constantly in everyone. *Repression*, or the "burying" process, was explained in Chapter 2. Repression is the process of "forgetting" certain kinds of experiences and information which may be too troublesome or painful to handle on a conscious level. Another mechanism, *sublimation*, is the process by which the basic drives are refined and directed into acceptable channels. Lyons, for example, sublimated much of his aggressive drive in his work.

3. A third group of mechanisms is made up of temporary

emergency devices, which are called into play automatically and selectively when there is some threat to the personality.

Denial, a form of repression, is one of these temporary devices. Suppose a plant superintendent has five years to go before reaching retirement age and his boss suggests that he pick a successor and train him. But our plant superintendent does not select a successor despite repeated requests from the boss. He cannot "hear" what the boss is saying. He may be forced to select such a man. When the time for retirement arrives, he may then say to his boss that the boss really did not intend to retire him. He cannot believe the boss will compel him to leave. This behavior reflects a denial of the reality of the situation because the ego has difficulty accepting what it regards to be a loss of love (status, esteem, and so forth).

Rationalization is another temporary mechanism that everyone uses from time to time. In fact, as the following example shows, it provides the subject matter for comedy!

A man's wife suggests that it is time to get a new car because theirs is already eight years old and getting shabby. At first, acting under the influence of the superego, the man doubts that he needs a new car. He cannot justify it to himself. To buy one without an adequate reason would be a waste of money. "You're too mature to be so extravagant and to fall for style," his superego says. The guilt aroused by the thought of buying a new car gives rise to anxiety, and the idea is rejected to appease the superego. The older car still runs well; it gives no trouble, and a new one would be expensive. Soon he enters an automobile showroom. "Just looking," he tells the salesman. "He thinks he's found a sucker," he chuckles to himself to avoid the condemnation of the superego. Next, however, he begins to complain to his wife and his friends that the old car will soon need repairs and that as time goes on, it will be worth less and less on a trade-in. Before long he has developed a complete rationale for buying the new car, and has convinced himself to do so.

Projection, another temporary mechanism, is the process of attributing to someone else what one himself feels. If, for example, one can project hostility onto someone else ("He's angry at me, he's out to get me."), then one can justify his hostility toward the other person ("It's all right for me to get him first.").

Idealization means glorifying someone else and thereby being unable to see his faults. This process is seen most vividly in people who are "in love" or who have identified strongly with political leaders. It enhances the image of the idealized person as a source of strength and gratification.

Reaction formation is a formidable term for doing the opposite of what one wants, to avoid the threat of giving rein to impulses. Some people become so frightened of their own aggressive impulses that they act in an extemely meek and mild manner, avoiding all suggestion of aggression.

Another important mechanism is *substitution,* or displacement. In this process the ego is unable to direct impulses to the appropriate target and directs them to a substitute target. This is what happens when a person who cannot give much affection to other people devotes it instead to his work. More destructive displacement occurs when a person seeks substitute targets for his aggression. Unable to express his anger with his superior, a man may displace it onto the working conditions or wages. Worse yet, he may unwittingly carry it home and criticize his wife or his children. This is the mechanism behind scapegoating and prejudice.

Compensation is still another mechanism and often a highly constructive one. This is the process of developing talents and skills to make up for one's deficiencies, or of undertaking activities and relationships to regain lost gratification. In certain respects, compensation and substitution are closely related.

These mechanisms need not be further elaborated here. It is enough to know that when the ego is threatened in some fashion, anxiety spontaneously and unconsciously triggers mechanisms to counteract the threat. If there are too many emergencies for the personality, it may then overuse these mechanisms, and this in turn will seriously distort the person's view of reality or cripple him psychologically. To identify with those one respects is not harmful; to imitate them slavishly is to lose one's individuality. It is a good thing to rationalize occasionally, as we all do, but it is not good to base judgments consistently on rationalizations.

By and large, self-fulfillment has to do with the ego's capacity to function as effectively as possible. When emotional conflicts can be diminished, when the need for defensiveness can be decreased, the energy that ordinarily maintains the defenses is freed for more useful activity. Furthermore, when, as threats are removed, the defenses need no longer be used, the person perceives reality more accurately. He then can relate to other people more reasonably and can communicate more clearly. A psychological blossoming-out can occur.

When balancing fails to take place, the ego is momentarily overwhelmed. Bob Lyons acted to relieve his emotional pain and killed himself before equilibrium could be restored.

CHAPTER 4

The Balancing Process

FUNDAMENTALLY, THE EGO HAS FOUR MODES OF CARRYING ON its balancing process. We therefore have a wide range of behavior possibilities with which to carry on the balancing task. The four basic balancing modes, the behavior that characterizes them, and their consequences could be schematized as follows:

Modes	*Behavior*	*Consequences*
1. Channeling the Drives	Fusion of Drives toward Appropriate Target	Problem Solution
2. Diverting the Drives	Displacement to Less Appropriate Target	Partial Problem Solution
3. Containing the Drives	"Sitting on" Drives	Psychosomatic Symptoms; Emotional Coldness
4. Reversing the Drives	Displacement onto the Self	Hurting Oneself; Self-Centeredness

The first mode is the most constructive. The second serves

to drain off tension (reduce the drive pressure and the need for maintaining defenses at a high level). It is therefore useful in the sense that it leaves the ego somewhat more flexible. However, since the ego is directing its energies to a substitute target, rather than to the one on which it should be working, this is not the most useful way of solving emotional problems. The third and fourth modes produce psychological symptoms. They are emergency ways of coping with anxiety. The more frequently the second, third, and fourth modes are used, the greater is the imbalance with which the ego is struggling, and the less efficient the ego is.

THE DESTRUCTIVE DRIVE

1. *Channeling the Drive (Fusion of Drives toward Appropriate Target; Problem Solution)*. Suppose a man is called into his superior's office and his superior criticizes him harshly for something he did not do. The ideally healthy man, if he exists, will listen calmly to his superior and, in good control of his rising aggressive impulse, may reply, "I'm sorry that such a mistake has happened. I had nothing to do with that particular activity, but perhaps I can help you figure out a way to keep the same mistake from happening again." His superior, also brimming with good mental health, may then respond, "I'm sorry that I criticized you unfairly. I would appreciate your giving me a hand on this." Together they direct their energies toward the solution of the problem.

2. *Diverting the Drive (Displacement to Less Appropriate Target; Partial Solution)*. But take a similar situation where the man knows his superior will brook no contradiction or is so emotionally overwrought that there is little point in trying to be reasonable with him. This man may fume with

conscious anger at the unjust attack, but he will control his impulse to strike back. He takes the criticism, anticipating a better solution when the superior cools off. Nevertheless, he is unconsciously angry for being unjustly criticized, and there is no opportunity to discharge his aroused aggressive impulse in an appropriate way toward the solution of the problem. Because it seems so rational to control one's impulse in the situation (that is, the superior is upset and there is no point in discussing it with him now), the ego finds this unconscious anger an inappropriate feeling to allow into consciousness. The more primitive unconscious anger is repressed. When the employee goes bowling that night he gets particular pleasure from knocking the pins down, without knowing why. Unconsciously he is using bowling to drain off his excess aggression. Such a displacement is a partially constructive way of discharging aggression: It hurts no one; it provides gratification. However, it does not contribute directly to resolving the problem itself.

3. *Containing the Drive ("Sitting on" the Drive; Psychosomatic Symptoms).* Suppose that another man finds himself in the same situation. This man has learned in the course of growing up that it is not permissible to express one's aggression directly to authority figures. Being human, he has aggressive impulses, but because he has a severe superego, he feels guilty about them and goes to great lengths to repress them. When the superior criticizes him, and his aggressive impulse is stimulated, automatically repression sets in and the impulse is controlled without his being aware of it. However, it is so controlled that he cannot speak up to contribute to the solution of the problem.

Because this man constantly maintains a high degree of control to meet the demands of his superego, he is already in a potentially more explosive situation, ready to defend himself from the slightest possible threat. If he has to contain more of his anger within himself, we have a situation that is much like rising steam pressure in a boiler. If this situation is repetitive or chronic, the mobilization and remobilizaton of defenses almost requires of the ego that it be in a steady emergency state. This kind of reaction strains the ego's resources and is particularly wearing physiologically because each psychological response to stress is accompanied by physical manifestations.

The result is usually a psychosomatic symptom. The body is literally damaged by its own fluids, leading to ulcers, hypertension, and similar phenomena. Clinical data seem to show that there are reasons why one particular organ is the site for a psychosomatic symptom, but often these reasons are obscure.

4. *Reversing the Drive (Displacement onto the Self; Hurting Oneself)*. Take still another man. This one has learned also that aggression should not be expressed to others, and he cannot do so without feelings of guilt. In fact, his superego will not tolerate much hostility on his part, so he lives constantly with feelings of guilt. The guilt, in turn, makes him feel inadequate as his superego repeatedly berates him for his hostility. No matter how nice he may try to be, he cannot satisfy his superego. Somehow, he himself always seems to be at fault. With such a rigid, punitive superego, this man under an attack may say, "I guess you're right. I'm always wrong; it's my fault. I never seem to do things right." He may also then have a mild depression. Depression is generally an indication of anger with oneself, originating from anger toward another, and reflects the attack of the superego on the ego. The aggression is displaced from the appropriate target back onto the self and results in a form of self-blame and self-punishment.

Another form of self-attack or self-punishment is seen in many accidents. Most accidents do not occur by chance, but are unconscious modes of self-punishment. The "forgetting" to turn the motor switch off before repairing the machine, or not seeing or hearing a possible threat, are frequently indications that denial or repression has been operating in order to permit the person to hurt himself to appease his own superego. In extreme form, this self-directed aggression is the mechanism behind suicide. This applied to Bob Lyons. Driven by an extremely severe superego, Bob Lyons sublimated his drives successfully in his work as long as he could work hard. By driving himself, he could appease the relentless pressure of his superego.

Such a superego, however, is never satisfied. Its demands arise from unconscious sources, which are to a large extent irrational. If they were not irrational, their terms could be met.

Whenever he reached a goal toward which he had aspired, Lyons could get no satisfaction from it, for his superego still drove him. And when he could no longer work as hard as he had, for him this was an environmental deprivation. His superego became more relentless. The vacation, with no demands on him at all, simply added to his guilt, to his feelings of unworthiness and inadequacy. With sublimations and displacements reduced, his aggressive drive had only his ego as a major target. And at that moment, the only way that Bob Lyons knew to appease his superego was to kill himself.

We can never know exactly why Bob Lyons committed suicide when he did. We can speculate on a range of possibilities, however.

It is reasonable to assume, at least in Western cultures, that no one would take his life unless he felt he had no alternative solutions to his problems. Lyons could have despaired for many reasons. He might have been fearful, perhaps unconsciously afraid of success, and each achievement might have increased his fear. Or, conversely, he might have been afraid of failure, and increasing achievement may then have threatened to make each possibility of failure that much more devastating. He might have experienced some important psychological loss as he rose in rank—perhaps the loss of friends and colleagues left behind on whom he had depended, or the inability to use methods for coping with his problems which he had used successfully before. If there were such losses, he could have felt deprived, lonely, and helpless. He may have had a growing feeling that others did not want him to succeed, however irrational such a feeling might have been, and that he would get even with them by destroying himself. He might have felt the press of growing anger which mounted to such intensity that he would have hurt someone else if he did not destroy himself first. Or he might have felt exploited by others against whom he felt he could not defend himself.

Apparently, having achieved what by cultural standards was success, that achievement meant nothing to him because he did not have a cohesive sense of himself as an individual and what he wanted to do in life. If, as we inferred, much of his life-long effort was an unconscious attempt to please his parents, his motivation derived from what he presumed they wanted rather than what he himself wanted. Under such circumstances, Bob Lyons could never be himself. What then would be the use of living?

Lyons probably derived little happiness from his many activities because of his sense of being driven. Conceivably, if he found life to be not much fun, despite his achievement, he might wonder why he should keep trying. Or having reached middle age and professional success without being able to enjoy what he had attained, he might have seen no possibility of subsequently finding gratification. Or, feeling that he had achieved all of his goals, what was left for him to do in life, particularly since his whole life had been directed to achieving goals and "doing"?

Many other speculations for which we have no clues are possible. We know nothing about his aspirations to achieve a more responsible position which for some reason now seemed impossible and therefore made him feel that he had failed. Although the information we have about his family relationships is positive, we have only a superficial picture of them. And what foreboding threat did aging hold for this vigorous man?

Many people struggle with these and similar problems for a lifetime and do not give up as Lyons did. Why some continue the struggle and others yield at some particular point we do not know. It is this unknown or "X" factor which makes diagnosis of suicidal risk difficult even for the expert.

This much we do know. Dr. Karl Menninger points out that some suicides are accidental, some are substitutes for murder, some are a cry for help, some are miscarriages of an attempt to get oneself rescued, and some are expressions of total despair. "It [suicide] expresses a suffering so terrible, a hopelessness so great, that only one resolution pervades the mind."*

Any one of a thousand transient events, and more likely some particular combination of those events, could have been the straw that broke Lyons' psychological back. Most of them would have seemed relatively unimportant to the outsider but they must have assumed huge proportions in Lyons' complex inner world—it is this inner world of man

* Karl Menninger, *The Vital Balance* (New York: The Viking Press, 1963), p. 268.

that we shall try to understand a little better in this book.

Had his superego been developed differently, Lyons might have achieved his goals because of ego reasons (the pleasure and gratification he got from his work), with a mild assist from the superego to do well (aspiration). When his superego developed so strongly, probably because of a heavy burden of hostility in childhood for which he felt irrationally guilty for a lifetime, there was no real pleasure in what he did and nothing more than temporary gratification. The relentless driving of himself was a form of self-sacrifice, just as are alcoholism, most accidents, repeated failures on the job, presenting the worst side of one's self to others, and some forms of crime.

We should recognize that there is a bit of this in everyone. There is a self-destructive potential in each person. Bob Lyons differed only in degree and only because of a combination of forces at a given point, which precipitated his death. A change in any single force might conceivably have prevented it: more and harder work, psychiatric treatment, no vacation to add to the feelings of guilt and uselessness, or open recognition by his physician of the seriousness of mental illness.

THE CONSTRUCTIVE DRIVE

The ego must deal with the *constructive* drive, as well as the aggressive drive, to maintain the proper balance. The same mechanisms that are used to cope with the aggressive drive apply themselves to handling the constructive drive, and in so doing, often cause a person distress as well as relief:

1. *Channeling the Drive (Fusion of Drives toward Appropriate Target; Problem Solution).* When fused with the aggressive drive, and dominant over it, the constructive drive

is directed toward appropriate targets in intimate relationships with one's family, the solution of work and family problems, and so on. Idealistic love without an aggressive component might lead to fantasied images of a sweetheart rather than marriage, or a person might dream about job success rather than acting toward it.

2. *Diverting the Drive (Displacement to Less Appropriate Target; Partial Solution).* As may the aggressive drive, the constructive drive may be deflected from appropriate targets. Homosexuality is one such phenomenon whose dynamics are too complex for discussion here. In brief, the homosexual cannot establish adequate and satisfying relationships with those of the opposite sex. Instead, he uses the mechanism of substitution and builds up extended rationalizations to appease his superego.

Some people can invest themselves in causes, but not really in other people. Some lavish great affection on animals or houses or hobbies at the expense of personal relationships. Some adults can have affectionate relationships only with young children and cannot tolerate other adults. These targets provide useful channels for love, but not the fully satisfying wide range of relationships enjoyed by most mature adults.

3. *Containing the Drive ("Sitting on" the Drive; Emotional Coldness).* Some people, for complicated reasons, feel it is psychologically safe not to express affection and have repressed their affectionate feelings. They seem without emotion. They may be highly intellectual or professionally successful, but they have divorced compassion from judgment and feeling from reasoning. Others are ruthlessly efficient. They keep their emotions tightly controlled and their feelings of love deeply buried.

4. *Reversing the Drive (Displacement onto the Self; Self-*

Centeredness). Children rejected by their parents learn bitterly that it is too painful to try to love other people because they will not return love. In adult life, such people become highly self-centered. In conversation they are constantly talking about themselves. They give overmeticulous attention to their appearance and revel in self-display. They tend to seek out activities that provide public adulation, and they become extremely unhappy when they cannot get it. We find such people unpleasant to deal with. Often they exploit others for their own gain. They have almost no real friends and often are unable to sustain their marriages.

For these people, much of the constructive drive is displaced onto themselves because environmental forces have made identification and introjection difficult, thereby impairing the possibility of relationships with other people. The early conflicts, now repressed, still exist unconsciously for the person. With its memories of early pain, the ego will not open itself again to the possibility of rejection and narrowly constricts the constructive drive to a limited target, to protect itself. Because of the limited range of attachments the ego permits, such people do not really enjoy life, despite what appears to others to be an extremely sparkling series of social adventures.

Each person must have a certain amount of self-love if he is to have self-respect. Overweening egocentricity, however, is ultimately destructive because of the absence of gratification, because of the pain caused other people, and because it diverts energy from social contributions the person could make.

An extreme form of egocentricity is hypochondriasis. Some people invest all their energy in being preoccupied with their own bodies. They are never free of aches and pains, and often spend years and untold dollars for "doctoring." They sacrifice most of life's pleasures to nurse their fancied ills, undeterred by repeated medical reports that show there is no need for surgery or that they do not have cancer.

In some respects, such people commit slow suicide as they cut themselves off more and more from the outside world. In some cases, such persons will even allow one or more limbs to atrophy from disuse because they claim it is too painful to walk or to move.

CAUTIONS

In Bob Lyons' case, we want to understand what happened to him, and how to apply this understanding to try to prevent similar tragedies. How would his colleagues, his wife, or his physician have recognized the early symptoms of his illness? It would not have been easy. It is impossible to put an ego under a microscope or locate the id in any part of the body. However, it is possible to describe some of the more common kinds of behavioral reactions to stress, so that you can more easily recognize symptoms of difficulty. And there are some steps you can take to relieve the stress you infer from the behavior you see. This will appear in Part II. But it is important that two cautions be raised.

First, the reader newly exposed to psychoanalytic theory invariably falls victim to the freshman medical student's syndrome: He gets every symptom in the book. The average reader will be able to see in himself everything to which this book refers. The reader should try to maintain an objective distance from the material.

The second caution has to do with the limitations of this exposition. This is necessarily a highly condensed version of some aspects of psychoanalytic theory. Many important aspects of the theory have been omitted; others have been presented without the many qualifications a serious scientific presentation would require. You should therefore look upon it only as an introduction to better understanding of the problems. You should be careful about overgeneralization and should studiously avoid using jargon or interpreting people's behavior to them. Within these limitations, you can render extremely important help. Unless you observe these precautions, you will be unable to help anyone.

FOR FURTHER READING

BRENNER, CHARLES. *An Elementary Textbook of Psychoanalysis.* New York: International Universities Press, 1955.

HALL, CALVIN S. *A Primer of Freudian Psychology.* New York: World, 1954.

MENNINGER, KARL A. *Man Against Himself.* New York: Harcourt Brace & Co. 1938.

REDLICH, FRITZ, and BINGHAM, JUNE. *The Inside Story.* New York: Alfred A. Knopf, Inc., 1953.

(*The above are also in paperback editions*)

ENGLISH, O. SPURGEON, and PEARSON, G. H. J. *Emotional Problems of Living.* New York: W. W. Norton & Company, Inc., 1955.

FREUD, ANNA. *The Ego and the Mechanisms of Defense.* New York: International Universities Press, 1946.

(*For first level supervisory training*)

MENNINGER, WILLIAM C., and LEVINSON, HARRY. *Human Understanding in Industry.* Chicago: Science Research Associates, 1956.

PART II

WHO'S SICK?

THE PERSONALITY HAS COMPONENTS THAT INTERACT WITH EACH other; it has several sources of energy: the constructive and destructive drives, and the energy of the ego. Like any other organized system, the personality has two functions: to maintain its integrity, and to carry on those activities for which it is destined by a combination of internal and external forces.

When either of these two functions is interfered with, that event is a conflict. A conflict arises when the two drives, love and hate, are opposed to each other; when an impulse arises that cannot be fulfilled because of superego constrictions or the requirements of reality; when external demands made on the ego cannot be met. Conflict results in some strain on the equilibrium of the personality and requires efforts to reestablish an equilibrium.

Not all conflict is bad, however; some is required for growth. Living is a constant process of conflict resolution. A person's preferred modes of dealing with threats or resolving conflicts become his enduring personality traits.

The process of coping with threat, in its most primitive form, has three sequential steps:

1. All resources—biochemical, physical, and psychological—are alerted by the mechanism of anxiety and make the person ready

49

to defend himself. Adrenalin pours into the blood stream. His digestion and other nonemergency functions are slowed while his heart beats faster to carry more oxygen to his brain. His muscles tense in anticipation of action. His thought processes are focused on the immediate problem, and almost all other stimuli are excluded from consciousness. He becomes hyperalert to all possible dangers. A person who is preoccupied or worried does not pay much attention to other happenings around him.

2. He adopts a defensive posture. He is ready to take some action. In fact, a common placating remark is, "Don't get your dander up."

3. He takes either of two types of action, fight or flight.

Although everyone has experienced this emergency defensive process, it is called a *symptom* when it is so severe or recurrent that it becomes disruptive to the personality. A symptom indicates that the person is making sometimes heroic, and usually painful, efforts to maintain an equilibrium.

Symptoms vary widely because each person has learned to cope with those problems peculiar to his own upbringing in ways that are most effective in his situation. In addition, as was indicated in the discussion of psychosomatic problems in Chapter 4, different parts of the body become preferred sites for physical symptoms for different people. This happens partly because those parts of the body seem to be the weakest links in the physiological chain for those people and partly because of the nature of the psychological conflict, to be discussed in Chapter 9.

Combinations of symptoms, called *syndromes,* are common enough that they have been organized into diagnostic categories. It is not necessary to learn these categories. Even psychiatrists and psychologists do not often put people into clear-cut categories. Rather, our purpose is to try to recognize and understand stress, and do something about it. Following are six different kinds of reaction patterns and the first-aid measures suitable for each case. In each one, the reaction pattern is not the whole of the person's behavior, but the most conspicuous facet of it.

In some instances, the mere understanding of what is going on and knowing that the person is trying to cope with some kind of threat will be enough to be helpful in resolving a problem. Such understanding may not alter what you do, but how you do it. You can be most helpful to people by making the task to be done the basis of your joint concern and by accepting the reality of the other person's feelings. When a person feels that someone understands how he feels, and at the same time is acting realistically, this is helpful to him.

Sometimes the most realistic action might be to move a man into a position that takes advantage of his behavior problem. Just because he has a problem that makes him unsuitable in one job does not mean that he is useless. With a little imagination, most organizations can turn a problem into a profit. For example, a person who becomes blind develops his other senses more keenly and might therefore be an unusual asset in many kinds of work.

Sometimes the most helpful action is discharge or referral to professional help. Referral will be discussed in Part IV. It is important to remember that though a person may not be able to change his behavior by himself, he is responsible for doing something about it if it interferes with his work. So, an important part of the process may well be to help people realize that something is wrong but that something can be done about it.

CHAPTER 5

Fear Reactions

A FEAR REACTION IS OFTEN CALLED "NERVOUSNESS" BY THE layman. It is a diffuse feeling of uneasiness. Often the person does not know why he is uneasy. He anticipates some kind of threat, and the ego has mobilized its resources to deal with the threat. In a simple fear reaction, a person has a feeling of restlessness and tension. He is unable to do his work as well as he is accustomed to doing it. He cannot organize his activities with the same efficiency. He has difficulty concentrating. In general, he cannot be so effective as he is ordinarily. Usually, he also has mild physical symptoms like diarrhea, palpitation of the heart, or stomach upsets.

This reaction reflects the suffusion of the personality with a hyperalert readiness to tackle potential danger. In a sense, the ego is prepared for an emergency with no place to go; that is, there is no specific symptom to which to attach the emergency energy and no specific way of resolving the conflict. Perhaps a good analogy is a group of firemen who have responded to a fire alarm but who cannot find the fire.

When there is a fear reaction without a clear indication of the source of the threat, usually the threat is an unconscious conflict.

A young man who was made assistant to the authoritarian president of a company became tense and jittery shortly afterward. He had looked forward to the promotion and he enjoyed his new work. In fact, he did not associate his symptoms with his new job. He did not know why he was upset, when ordinarily he was in reasonably good health. As he talked about his symptoms with his doctor, he saw that he was reacting in fright to the forbidding older man. When this became clear to him, he recognized that he need not be so frightened, and his symptoms disappeared.

The layman is not in a position to understand and interpret the reasons for a given fear reaction. You can, however, suggest to the person who is reacting this way that he try to think of what recent events may have created distress for him. You can also reassure the person by giving him an opportunity to talk, if he wants to, and by telling him that such reactions are quite common.

Fear reactions are often related to specific threatening situations. They are commonplace in almost any dangerous situation or in one that threatens loss of love. People who take their first airplane ride tend to have considerable fear, and even experienced passengers grow tense when the ride becomes bumpy. Pilots who have been accident-free may become fearful when they feel they have been lucky too long, and they view each additional flight as living on borrowed time. Children often have fear reactions when they feel tension between their parents. Fear reactions occur frequently, too, when unconscious impulses are stimulated. A man who has learned to control his aggressive impulses tightly may become anxious when an argument with a colleague stimulates him to the point where he feels his ego controls slipping.

In these situations, reassurance and support in the form of explanation, or a change in the situation (separating the two men), diminishes the threat to the point where the ego can cope with it. Any way in which the person can feel protected or can act to solve the conflict serves to diminish the anxiety.

ACUTE REACTIONS

When fear reactions are of more severe proportions, they usually require professional help. A person who is in a panic, or who seems to be so jittery that he cannot act for himself, has so much anxiety that his ego temporarily cannot function adequately. Someone else has to act in place of his ego or to give comprehensive support to the ego. Sedation is one form of relieving the ego of such anxiety. Hospitalization or some other form of external control is another mode of support.

A 32-year-old engineer was assigned an important role in a major project. He had had a successful career in his company up to this point, having done well on successive projects, and matured considerably. However, he had not previously had independent responsibility. After several weeks had passed on the new assignment, the engineer became "nervous." His colleagues knew that he had difficulty sleeping and that he was losing weight. Sometimes his hands trembled so badly that he dropped instruments with which he was working. In one unguarded moment he remarked, "I don't think I can stand it. I'm afraid I'll hurt myself or someone else." From time to time it seemed as if he had been crying. Upon the urging of his manager, he went to his family doctor. When sedatives did not relieve his symptoms, he was hospitalized. Hospitalization removed him from his difficult work situation, assured him of external controls and support, and gave him an opportunity to discuss and understand his problem. Thus strengthened, he was able to discuss his difficulties with the personnel officer, obtain a transfer, and continue treatment in the form of regular visits to a psychiatrist.

Unfortunately, too many people have a tendency to ignore the urgent plea for help that lies in the statement, "I'm afraid I'll hurt myself or someone else." It should not be disregarded. Such a remark indicates the need for professional help.

CHRONIC REACTIONS

When an emergency alarm reaction becomes chronic, either of two kinds of behavior or both, are likely to result: (1) Perhaps anxiety remains as a gross feature of behavior. In this case we commonly speak of the person as being "highly nervous." His tension, and over-responsiveness become characteristic of him. (2) The anxiety may become specifically channeled into one symptom. The symptom itself will be an effort to avoid or control the underlying impulse that is giving rise to the anxiety.

Some people, for example, are unconsciously so afraid of their own self-destructive impulses that they will not climb ladders. Others are afraid to get into automobiles, and still others are afraid to approach certain animals. They do not know why they have these fears, but the fears are specific enough that they cannot bring themselves to do the thing they fear. Many people are able to function well by simply avoiding what they have come to fear. A fairly common fear is the sight of blood. Those who have such a fear have no problem as long as they can avoid seeing blood. But the sight of it can make them physically ill.

A thirty-nine-year-old supervisor, who had been with his company thirteen years, reported to the company medical department with complaints of insomnia and fear that he had tuberculosis. He had a cough, which seemed to accompany a cold, but there were no other indications of illness. According to his superiors, he had been doing well on his job and had worked his way up to a responsible position. They observed, however, that he seemed to feel inferior, particularly in relationships with older men.

The supervisor told the physician that he was afraid he had tuberculosis as a result of fumes in the plant and that he was afraid he might lose his job. At the same time, he hoped to be promoted to a more responsible job. An older man in the plant who had helped him along the way had recently died. He did not know if he could handle his work himself, particularly since he was not getting much help from his boss. From time to time, he became angry with his boss, but he could not express his anger. When he became angry, he also became anxious. As soon as his anxiety diminished, he felt a pain in his chest and coughed. (The anxiety was transformed into a physical symptom.) Then he became frightened, thinking he had tuberculosis.

He was referred to a psychiatrist. In psychiatric interviews, it became apparent that the fear of tuberculosis was a way of managing the anxiety aroused by his anger toward the boss. The fear was also related to similar illnesses in two close relatives when he was a child, one of whom had died from the illness. When the relationship between his symptom and his anger was pointed out, his tension decreased. Reassurance of his value to the plant further decreased his anxiety, particularly after the plant physician advised his boss to recognize his need for encouragement and support.

Some weeks later, he said to the physician, "I don't know what you fellows did, but things are certainly different around here." His work continued to be satisfactory, although occasionally he needed additional reassurance from the physician that he was in good health.

Many people deal with fears by attempts to overcontrol themselves or their environment. By being extremely orderly in what they do, they try to head off threatening possibilities. Some adopt rituals of behavior they must perform as modes of control. For example, a young chemist became so preoccupied with the fear of contamination that he was almost constantly washing his hands. This symptom so interfered with his laboratory work that he had to give it up. Unconsciously he wanted to be dirty. His impulse to be dirty was intolerable in consciousness because of prohibitions he had learned as a child. Yet because he had such an impulse, he felt himself to be dirty, and sought to wash away the dirt. Of course the literal action of washing himself could not remove the unconscious impulse, and a man cannot continue to wash his hands without some seemingly rational reason. The fear of contamination provided both a rational reason and a figurative reference to the evil impulse.

DENIAL AS THE BASIS FOR PHYSICAL SYMPTOMS

One way of dealing with pressing anxiety is to use the defense mechanism of *denial*. The person tries to deny to himself that he is threatened. Denial, however, does not make the anxiety go away. It must still be dealt with, and the ego may do so by "attaching" the anxiety to a specific bodily organ. For example, a person may have a paralysis without having a physical impairment to account for it. Psychological paralysis of an arm might result from an unconscious impulse to strike some other person. The impulse is not acceptable in consciousness, yet the feeling is extremely strong and the ego defends itself by immobilizing the arm. This case is illustrative:

> A middle-aged, highly intelligent woman who was an advertising copywriter was the only person left in her family. She had few close friends in the large city in which she worked. She developed paralysis of both legs and had to use a wheel chair. Again, no physical basis was found for the symptom and all efforts to help her understand the psychological reason for it failed. She simply denied any relationship between her symptom and fears. But to recover from her symptom was to have to face the world alone again. That, apparently, she could not bring herself to do.

Effort to remove a symptom often results in increasing anxiety on the part of the person because the symptom represents the best way he can come to terms with the psychological threat. The symptom is a less effective way of dealing with the disequilibrium than many other ways might be. It is nevertheless the best way for that person at that particular time. Symptoms are always the result of multiple causes and represent a balancing of forces within the personality. Thus their origins are complex. The more complex the network of forces producing a particular symptom, the more difficult it is to eliminate the symptom.

The complexity of just one aspect of the origin of the symptom is easily seen. For example, there are hundreds of ways of dealing with loneliness. Some people are so adept in their relationships that they never feel lonely. But many others continue to be lonely because they are unable to establish or maintain continuing ties. The story of the man with many acquaintances but no friends is an old one.

Those alcoholics who are fighting off more serious illness by drinking may become depressed or so disorganized as to be irrational when they are denied access to liquor. A man who was hospitalized for months for low back pain became severely disorganized when his pain was removed by hypnosis. He no longer had a legitimate reason for being in the hospital and was unable to face the psychological problems that made being a patient the best way he could adjust to life.

Clinicians therefore usually do not attempt to remove a symptom directly, but try to influence those forces that make the patient "choose" a particular symptom. Thus they try to help the patient find less costly, more effective ways of dealing with his problems. Such symptoms as physical impairments indicate a need for psychological treatment (psychotherapy), always in conjunction with medical treatment so that the function of the affected limb will not be lost. Even though the woman patient previously discussed could not walk by herself, she was still helped to exercise her legs each day and was given physiotherapy.

PERSONALITY TYPES

When a defense mechanism becomes so overused as to be the person's most important mode of adaptation, it becomes a fixed personality trait. The person who unconsciously adopts *avoidance* (a form of repression) as a characteristic mode of adjustment typically tries to avoid expressing his own emotions and committing himself to a course of action. Such people are often insensitive to the feelings of others and cover their relationships with a torrent of words. Others tend to see them as "cold." For example, an executive of the subsidiary of a large merchandising company was described this way by one of his superiors:

> He has excellent business abilities. He can analyze and organize figures very quickly. He has strong competitive drive and persistence to go with it. He is very industrious in his day-to-day activities and he is especially alert to cutting costs, something he can do without regard for the feelings of the people involved. At the same time he is unable to make decisions without many doubts. He is unable to take responsibility and this inability goes to the extent of actually lying about a situation when it serves his purpose. He is subservient to his superiors and demands the same kind of subservience from his subordinates. He views each problem in the organization within the narrow perspective of its effect on himself. He cannot delegate responsibility. He has no sense of humor and almost no regard for human dignity. His subordinates who have responsibility for labor relations, personnel practices, and similar matters seem unable to develop rapport with this man, and because of their fear of their boss, with other line executives who are his subordinates.

The *overcontrolled* style of adaptation has some of the same cold emotional qualities. The ego has a tight and guarded hold on impulses in response to a highly demanding superego. Instead of indecision we find inflexibility from a rigidly held course of action and a tendency to be concerned with petty detail. A vice-president describes this kind of a traffic manager:

Over the many years he has been with the company his attendance has been good, though he usually arrives late and stays late—has not taken a vacation in years. He likes to chat with fellow employees and others who come to his office, yet at times he is blunt or rude to both. There is a problem in getting him to perform his job efficiently, though his long experience should qualify him. He does not put first things first, often failing to meet deadlines of the utmost importance. When given an important assignment with a deadline, he performs his less important routine work before starting the urgent assignment. He is a stickler for unnecessary and detailed paper work. Outwardly he appears to be loyal and interested, with a feeling of security and some importance. He has very few outside interests other than occasional fishing. He seems set and satisfied with his way of doing things, though his detailed procedures retard his work. I have attempted to confer with him at various times for the purpose of eliminating the unnecessary details, but he always indicates that at that time he has too much to do for the conference to be successfully completed. Though I have asked him to let me know when he feels he has enough time to continue, he has yet to do so.

Neither of these men was psychologically able to carry the tasks to which he had been assigned because, despite the outward appearance of efficiency, neither was really efficient in the performance of his job. With close supervision and limited functions, both would have made excellent staff men. As it was, both had to devote too much strength to permanent defensive activities—temporary defense mechanisms had become permanent for them. This implies that they had few other defensive devices to fall back on, and therefore they had few resources for changing their behavior. Certainly, nothing that any supervisor might do could enable these men, or others like them, to change. When a single defense mechanism has become such a dominant part of the personality, only intensive psychological treatment will have any effect, and often even that will yield only limited results.

Those who adopt *denial* as a major mode of adaptation do not permit themselves the freedom to look deeply into themselves or to be moved by their own thoughts and feelings. Psychologically, the ego tries to prevent any stimuli from penetrating so deeply as to evoke repressed memories. This is done by responding very quickly to many external stimuli. Such people are often seen as "flighty" or immature. They seem to respond too much to external stimuli. Other people may laugh at a joke; to them, it is uproarious. They tend to act impulsively and to be unable to involve themselves deeply with other people. Their energies are so tied up in their repressive defenses and in their hyperreadiness to respond to outside stimuli that they cannot make effective use of their capacities. Their thinking is shallow. They are too ready to agree with others or to avoid serious matters by making a joke of them.

Those who avoid their own feelings tend to become highly abstract and overintellectual, as if to reject the necessity for feelings. Those who overcontrol themselves tend to do the same by their preoccupation with details and organization. In contrast, the person who uses denial as his major mode of adjustment cannot sustain tension (delay impulses) long enough to make good decisions (abstract) or organize his work in detail (control). As a result, he cannot think deeply or sense the emotional quality of a situation. He is therefore not noted for his judgment. More often, he appears naive.

Such a man is described by the president of a public utility company:

A bright thirty-four-year-old division manager is difficult to supervise because he does not delve into problems deeply enough to come up with good solutions. He has a tendency to make snap decisions based on superficial review of the facts. Consequently our communication has had to be one of detailed questioning and establishment of tentative solutions before making decisions. All of this is upsetting to the man, since he is impatient to come up with an answer. He feels that we are indecisive. In addition, he has the habit of making sharp remarks in an attempt to be humorous. This has happened in important business conferences with governmental and financial representatives. These outside people have not taken kindly to his remarks, and we have had to smooth things over on several occasions. Also as a result of these remarks, some of our important customers are reluctant to trust him with confidential information. Some improvement has followed conferences with him about these matters, but the lack of deep, penetrating analysis continues to bother me because I cannot delegate jobs which should be handled by this man.

This man is unlikely to become the penetrating analyst his supervisor wants, at least not without professional help. His brightness is a reflection of potential, not performance. He will not attain his potential because he cannot delay his impulses long enough to choose a proper course of action. He reacts too quickly, and therefore inappropriately, to the pressure of his superior's demands and to the presence of the visiting officials (authority figures). While he may make slight improvements by conscious efforts, such denial has become his style of life, no significant change is to be expected without treatment. He should be in a job, therefore, whose requirements would be satisfied with superficialities: casual contacts with others who are not in authority over him and no decisions that have to be based on reflective thinking. Some forms of selling would probably be more in keeping with his psychological limitations.

CHAPTER 6

Depressive Reactions

DEPRESSIVE REACTIONS, NEXT TO FEAR REACTIONS, ARE PROB-ably the most common of all psychological symptoms. Depression is a sense of dejection, pessimism, low spirits. Depression has three origins, all of which stimulate anger with oneself as well as other feelings:

1. When a person has experienced a severe loss as a result of which deeply felt dependent wishes are stimulated and have no source of gratification. He can neither give nor receive affection as he could before his loss. The loss may be of a person, as through death, or it may be a change in job (promotion, transfer, discharge). The feeling tone is one of desperation.

2. When a person is stimulated to strong aggressive impulses for which he has no acceptable outlet or which are severely repressed, he may turn these against himself. Bob Lyons was a case in point. The feeling is one of fearfulness.

3. When the urge to love someone else or be loved is stimulated and there are no suitable avenues of gratification. Guilt and shame are the characteristic feelings.

Many events in our culture contribute to depressive feelings. Chapter 2 discussed the development of the self-critical functions of the superego, particularly in middle-class Western families. Disappointment in oneself is a cultural hazard when the culture places heavy emphasis on achievement and success. When families are tight-knit, the departure of children for their own adult lives sometimes leaves the parents with an acute sense of loss. The increasing use of labor-saving devices leaves many people with less to do physically, sometimes with an accompanying sense of uselessness and therefore increased guilt feelings. In short, there are many forces that deprive us of the opportunity to love and be loved and which make us angry with ourselves.

ACUTE REACTIONS

Sooner or later almost everyone loses someone he loves. In addition to the sense of loss, mourning often includes the feeling that one could have and should have been "better" to the deceased. Thus a mourner feels that he has lost something of himself, he is not so good as he should be, and he criticizes himself for his hostility to the other person. Here we see evidences of guilt feelings aroused by the superego.

Because these experiences are so widely shared, each person can understand the depressed mood of the mourner. Most of us can also understand the feeling of defeat a person has when he loses his job, or when he falls short of some public goal toward which he made strenuous efforts, such as an athletic championship.

Another experience of depression is more common, but is less widely shared. That is the sense of anger with and disappointment in ourselves when we do not live up to our standards or when we make some foolish error. Almost everyone has had such feelings at one time or another, but it is usually difficult to understand why someone else should feel so "low" at any given time. The fact that a person would behave in ways that others regard as overreacting suggests that whatever problem he is dealing with is more important to him than others realize. When the overreaction takes the form of depression, we can usually infer that the problem has to do with superego standards.

In all these circumstances, there is a precipitating event. But in some depressions, no precipitating event is evident; it is unconscious and unseen. A person simply becomes increasingly depressed without knowing why. Such a reaction reflects mounting unconscious conflict.

Next to fear, depression is probably the most frequent feeling of distress. As a transient symptom, it is extremely widespread. As a result, we have developed intuitive first-aid devices. When a death occurs in a family, friends gather around. They help with many details, bring food, comfort the bereaved. In effect, they replace the lost love temporarily with demonstrations of love until the bereaved can recover from his loss.

When someone tells us of a "stupid" mistake about which he feels angry with himself, often the sympathetic listener will describe an even more stupid mistake he made. Thus he helps appease the superego of the other person by showing that the mistake was a commonplace and not worthy of harsh internal judgment. Or when a person seems to be depressed, a friend may simply put his arm around the man's shoulders. This simple human touch tells the person without words that his friend has regard and affection for him, thus helping to restore his self-esteem.

Crying is a common reaction in grief and mourning as well as in other forms of depression. Our first response in such situations usually is to try to help the person stop crying. You can be far more helpful to such a person by letting him cry, particularly if you sit quietly by to indicate that you understand his feelings and that his tears are neither an inappropriate nor unusual reaction to such feelings.

This is one reaction, however, that is not helped by over-attentive affection. Support can be simple and direct, as in the examples above. It may also be in the form of distracting the person from his preoccupation by inviting him to take part in activities into which he can channel his aggressive impulses. Gross physical activity, as in chores, bowling, golf and other muscular pastimes, and those activities that serve other people's needs, are particularly helpful.

Gross physical activity helps divert the person's attention from preoccupation with himself, directs his aggressive impulses away from himself in ways that also provide enjoyment, and helps to maintain his physical well being. Service to others increases his self-esteem and relieves some of the pressure of the superego.

CHRONIC REACTIONS

Depression becomes an illness when it goes beyond a transient feeling of inadequacy and loss of self-esteem or when a person does not recover from a mourning period with the passage of time. By the time that symptoms of depression become so severe as to be an illness, we are seeing a chronic reaction. Some authorities assert that the average attack lasts from six to eighteen months, and in some cases, a chronic low-level depression may continue for years. Although depression can occur at almost any age period, it is most frequent following events that bring about major psychological changes in a person's life: graduation, childbirth, promotion, retirement, loss of a valued friend. It occurs more often after the age of thirty and is usually accompanied by a host of physical symptoms. In fact, sometimes the physical symptoms are so much more conspicuous that they mask the depressive feelings.

Chronic depressive reactions are marked by difficulty in sleeping; loss of appetite and weight; a dejected, defeated, exhausted tone; slowing down of speech and activities; and concern about physical symptoms. In addition, people who have such reactions are likely to be irritable, to have weeping spells, and to be preoccupied with their own behavior. Often, people with depressive reactions go to their physicians for treatment of their physical symptoms. Frequently, neither they nor the physician recognize the underlying depression. Often, when the stresses that precipitated the reaction have passed, they make a spontaneous recovery. With recurrent stress, however, they become depressed again.

Depressed people often feel heavily weighted down by their own responsibilities and the demands of the outside world. Their emotional sluggishness reflects their fatigue as a result of devoting so much energy to defenses. Here is an example in which the symptoms are relatively generalized:

A man in his late twenties was in excellent health when employed by his company. Just a few years later, in the fall of 1950, he reported to the company medical director that he was not able to sleep and felt weak. By the spring of 1951, he had lost nine pounds and still was not sleeping well. He was tense and unable to relax. He felt the pounding of his heart and throbbing in his abdomen. The company physician felt he was suffering from an emotional disturbance and referred him to an internist who prescribed a vacation.

There was temporary relief from the insomnia during the vacation but it recurred afterwards. The internist now recognized and treated depressive symptoms. In the summer of 1951, he took his regular vacation and felt much better on his return to work. In January, 1952, he was given a physical examination, at which time he reported that he "felt like a different person" compared to the way he had felt a year before. He still suffered from insomnia and took sedatives each night. In six months he gained sixteen pounds. But he was still tense and still had a tremor in his fingers, which had been present a year and a half before.

Two years later on examination he was considered well, but the next year some of the same symptoms were apparent again. He became irritable, indecisive, and quarrelsome. He looked tired, but he had not lost much weight. Again a vacation was prescribed. The symptoms diminished somewhat over the next year.

By 1957, they recurred. The physician noted that he was trying hard to be cheerful, but that his voice was a monotone. This time he was given psychiatric treatment in a hospital, after which he returned to work, sleeping well, and was in good spirits. Two years later, on examination, he was feeling well and had no complaints. He had been working full time and was no longer taking sedatives or tranquilizers.

In this case, the physicians recognized depression, but temporized with it over a seven-year period, to the discomfort of the man and the organization. Perhaps they would not have postponed definitive treatment if the symptoms had been as sharply focused as in the following case:

A thirty-eight-year-old woman personnel clerk complained of fatigue and depression. She withdrew from family and friends, preferring to be alone. When interviewed by her physician, she would cry on the slightest provocation, after which she was very much embarrassed for having done so. Insomnia became a problem. She compared her situation to being caught in a spider web with no avenue of escape. She was referred for psychiatric treatment and was able to return to her job five months later. She married some months afterward and continued to maintain her health.

Severe depressions are marked by inability to work, extended crying, suicidal thoughts and impulses, false ideas of having made mistakes, and sometimes even hearing criticizing voices. A particularly critical time for severe depressions in men is the so-called involutional period of the late fifties and early sixties, when they may have difficulties facing the problems of aging. Women in menopause frequently have the same feelings of helplessness, uselessness, and impending death. People with severe depressions are always potentially suicidal and should be carefully watched. All chronic and severe depressions require treatment, and most patients respond well to therapy. The following case shows how a man's superiors were an important complement to a treatment program:

This man was thirty-six and came from a strict fundamentalist family. His father was successful and overbearing. He left home to join the air force during World War II after a year in college. He was not able to qualify as a pilot. When he returned from service, he quarreled with his parents about his prospective wife. Then he married her and obtained a job in a large organization. When he was moved to a distant city for part of his training, which required that he be rotated from one place to another, he was separated from his family. In addition, all the men who were training him were much more specialized than he, which stimulated feelings of inadequacy.

He developed "jitters," depression, a fear of others' opinion of his behavior, fear of his inability to do his job, and a desire to throw himself out the window. He was admitted to a hospital for treatment. While he was in the hospital, he was visited frequently by his department heads. They talked to him frankly about their investigation of his capacity before they had hired him. They reassured him strongly about their knowledge of his abilities. When he left the hospital, they arranged for him to spend time with his family before returning to his training. He completed his training successfully and then went on to a responsible, relatively independent job in the organization. His superiors, recognizing his fears of failure, by swift and sympathetic support created an atmosphere in which he could function effectively.

MECHANISMS OF DEPRESSION

The major mechanisms of depression are *repression* and *displacement*. A depressed person is angry with someone other than himself, but he has repressed the idea that he is angry at the other person and displaces his feelings to himself. He feels he is unworthy of love. His strenuous efforts at work are often both a way of earning love and of relieving his guilt feelings for his unconscious hostility toward the person he believes should have loved him. Often, too, when a man experiences a depression after attaining some success, it is as if he is breaking a tie with important loved ones in his past. For example, a man who comes from humble origins may unconsciously feel that each promotion takes him so much farther from his parents. Finally, a major upward step makes it clear he can never return to them.

A man who feels unworthy of the esteem of others may become depressed when promoted, feeling convinced that he does not deserve promotion. Another man with strong unconscious feelings of rivalry toward his father or brother, which are unacceptable to his superego, may feel guilty and therefore may become depressed if promotion, in his mind, means vanquishing his rival. For still others, promotion may mean that there are no more goals to conquer, and therefore no further ways to appease the superego. Of course such feelings are unconscious and therefore irrational. But they exist as strong motivating forces nevertheless.

SUICIDE

This discussion of the dynamics of personality began with a case of suicide. Suicide is a more pressing problem than most people realize. According to the best available figures, some 19,000 people commit suicide each year. But these statistics are incomplete, for some suicides are not reported as such, and the man who kills himself by ramming his automobile into a tree rarely leaves an explanation behind.

It is particularly important that people in executive ranks recognize the seriousness of this problem because suicide occurs more frequently among educated middle- and upper-class men with high aspirations than among women (although there are more suicidal attempts among women) and lower-class men, and the suicide rate increases with age.

Suicide prevention clinics have been established in some

of the larger metropolitan areas. They are listed in local telephone directories and provide twenty-four hour professional help to people who are threatening suicide. Among these are the Los Angeles Suicide Prevention Center; the San Francisco Suicide Prevention Center; Rescue, Inc., of Boston; the Friends in Miami; and the National Save-a-Life League in New York. The League has representatives in other communities as well as New York, and 2,500 people seek its help each year.

Often suicide can be prevented, but sometimes it cannot be prevented even by the most careful efforts. Unfortunately, there is no way of knowing for certain whether a person intends to kill himself, but there are certain conditions under which suicide is more likely to occur, and these can serve as warning signs:

1. When he is deeply depressed and expresses feelings of helplessness and futility
2. When he has continued to be without appetite, continued to lose weight, and does not seem to care much about what happens to him
3. When he tries to cover up suicidal thoughts
4. When he makes an extremely rapid recovery from depression, suggesting that perhaps he has made a decision that will resolve his problem. (The reader cannot know whether recovery from depression is genuine. Such a judgment should be left to the professional, and sometimes even he will have difficulty making it.)
5. When in a deep depression he has false ideas and hears voices, reflecting the breakdown of the ego
6. When a person has a history of other suicidal attempts. (There is a critical ninety-day period after a person has been suicidal, during which time physicians and relatives should

be especially watchful. Suicidal attempts tend to recur during this period when the person appears to be improving.)

Suicidal thoughts are fairly common. Not everyone who thinks about suicide will kill himself, and some who are not depressed but suffer from other illnesses kill themselves. A suicidal phase is usually a temporary period. Precautions during that period are especially important. The layman should not try to determine whether a person might try to commit suicide, nor should he pass off a suicidal threat lightly. Rather, he should refer the person for professional help immediately and let the doctor decide what should be done. Most important of all, he should never make light of or try to laugh off anyone's fears about committing suicide. One of the heart-rending aspects of suicide is that so often the person tells someone else of his struggle and the other person fails to hear the cry for help.

PERSONALITY TYPES

People who have a depressive outlook on life tend to be hypersensitive to frustration. They seem more readily to develop feelings of hopelessness, pessimism, and futility. Sometimes, to counteract these feelings, they work very hard and drive themselves at a terrific pace, as did Bob Lyons. Sometimes, also, they are self-centered to make up for the love they feel they are not getting from their environment. Their extremely severe superegos not only make them have a strong sense of personal responsibility, but also make it impossible for them ever to live up to their expectations of themselves. As a result, they are always striving for perfection. They are therefore often very good employees and executives. They have very high standards for themselves and others, and they give themselves to the success of the organization. They tend to be quite inflexible, and sometimes they demand such a high performance of others that they lose their effectiveness as supervisors. They also tend to lose the affection and friendliness of others because of their high standards, depressed outlook, and self-centeredness.

Sometimes people who live with continuing depressive feelings go through cycles, now excitedly operating at a very fast pace, now sluggish in mood. Here is an example:

Andy Armstead is a senior executive whose swings in mood are so radical that his colleagues find it impossible to work with him. When he wishes to do so, he can turn on an extraordinary amount of charm (reaction formation) and can be a very pleasant colleague. His associates have come to appreciate his brilliant mind, especially when it comes to analyzing problems in which he is keenly interested.

Then, for no apparent reason (unconscious conflict), he will lose interest completely in business transactions, (depression) to the point of complete disregard for his own financial loss (self-punishment). At the same time, his personality will change so completely that he becomes a most obnoxious and disagreeable person (hostility, displacement). The mood might last as long as a month. Then there will be a short period of remorse (guilt), and finally he returns to his former level of extreme enthusiasm. His unpleasant and disagreeable moods, however, have become so frequent and so far outweigh his pleasant periods that he has lost all of his business associates and friends. The special problem he presents is that he is an extremely difficult person to whom to communicate one's thoughts and needs. He tends to think of his own wants and problems (self-centeredness) even while others are discussing theirs with him, and their points simply do not register with him (denial), even when they are for his particular benefit.

Those who maintain an intensive pace often appear to be running away from the threatening depression. Some do, in fact, keep moving from one place to another. Others start drinking to ward off such feelings. Still others operate in a quiet and almost withdrawn way, flat and colorless in their reactions and unassertive in their relationships. For them, life is not very exciting or even enjoyable.

Clinicians have long remarked on the fact that such an outlook, and even suicide, seems to repeat itself in families. Earlier generations of professionals therefore believed these reactions were the result of heredity. Some few still do. It it not difficult, however, to understand that if one or another parent has a depressive outlook on life or has extremely high standards, the children are likely to be reared under such conditions and to acquire the same personality dynamics. Thus personality styles and even symptoms can be transmitted psychologically from generation to generation.

When people do have depressive feelings, as most people do at one time or another, forced rest vacations should never be prescribed for them. Such vacations provide no outlet for the aggressive drives or relief from the guilt feelings. Vacations may increase the guilt feelings and the depression by making the person feel that he does not deserve the pleasure he is offered. Joyous holiday periods seem to be just the opposite for people who cannot enjoy life as others do. Their feelings of depression tend to increase as the Christmas holiday season nears.

For such people, also, lavish praise is difficult to live with. That, too, increases their guilt feelings, for they feel they do not deserve that much. Rather, matter of fact recognition of their achievements is psychologically better for them. They count heavily on the approval of others, but discount it when it goes beyond what they narrowly consider to be honest recognition.

CHAPTER 7

Withdrawal Reactions

_____

THE MOST CONSPICUOUS FORM OF FLIGHT IN THE FACE OF STRESS is withdrawal from other people. This takes the form of wanting to be alone, avoiding social contacts as much as possible, and in effect, pulling into one's "shell." There are times when people want to be alone, indeed need to be alone, to have privacy to think or to resolve a problem. Under those circumstances, a person readily returns to his friends. A withdrawal reaction, however, is more conspicuous because there seems to be no apparent reason for it, or the reasons given do not seem to justify the reaction or the degree of withdrawal, or its length seems disproportionate to the need.

Withdrawal becomes potentially malignant when the person cuts off his ties to his friends, colleagues, and his usual activities. Sometimes he does this abruptly; at other times he retreats from one person or activity at a time. Withdrawal under these conditions is usually a way of coping with pressing aggressive impulses. By withdrawing, the person invests all his energies in himself and begins to lose touch with the world around him. By the same token, he manages to protect himself against his hostility toward other people by repressing it severely and staying away from them.

The gradual loss of contact with others affects his responsiveness to them. Living within himself, the person begins to seem odd to others. He is no longer on the same wave length, as adolescents would put it. He seems to be on the outside of the social group, looking in. When a person loses contact with other people and limits his interactions with his environment, he loses some of the response of the environment, which is necessary for making a judgment. Since he needs some basis for judgment, in the absence of adequate and accurate information from outside himself, the person will have to construct a basis for action out of the information he has inside himself. He will tend to use *projection* and *rationalization* to make up for the information he does not have.

If a pressing internal problem for such people is their threatened loss of control over their hostility, it will be relatively easy for them to attribute their own hostility to other people and to believe that their own logic about a situation represents the facts. Everyone supplies his own "facts" when he does not have enough information about a situation. This is likely to happen consistently with people who have become withdrawn. The following case illustrates this behavior:

Rena Stone was for years an extremely competent senior secretary. Her husband was a widely respected attorney in their community, and her son was a high school sophomore. Rena did not need to work for financial reasons. She did so because she liked being in the business world and in the key position she held. Rena was known as a reticent woman who never spoke of what went on in her office; this, in addition to her evident competence, was what made her such a prized secretary.

As a matter of fact, Rena did not let herself be in situations where she could talk—not because of what she might say, but because that was the way she preferred it. Rena and her husband lived, for the most part, at home. On Sundays they would play golf with one other couple, their best friends. Only rarely did they accept social invitations, and even more rarely did they entertain small groups of close friends. Rena's husband avoided the official posts and community responsibilities which could have been his out of the respect people had for him.

When Rena's husband was killed in an automobile accident, people understood her burden. They did not call when it became apparent she felt overwhelmed by callers. As weeks went by, Rena did not return to work. She still did not want to see anyone. People heard from those few callers she did see that she did not want to be pitied. She was bitter because her husband had died while other, older men lived. She felt those who were trying to be kind to her were doing so out of a sense of obligation and not because they really cared about her. As soon as she could settle her affairs, she moved to a distant community.

ACUTE REACTIONS

In the preceding case, the withdrawal occurred in response to a specific precipitating event. It was simply an accentuation of the person's ordinary way of behaving. Until her husband's death, Rena Stone was a somewhat isolated person, but well within the acceptable range of behavior. She was respected for her effective work, maintained a good home life for her family, and minded her own business.

Another form of withdrawal is somewhat more puzzling. Here it is evident that changes in circumstances have something to do with the man's behavior, but his withdrawal seems to be more severe than the circumstances warrant. In short, he is overreacting, reflecting the fact that however mild the change may seem to others, it touches something deeply personal within him.

A department manager who had worked his way up in the organization had more than thirty years of service with his firm, fifteen in his present job. After a new management took over the plant, it became apparent that the manager was an ineffective supervisor. He lived near the plant; yet, he arrived late. He took an exceedingly long lunch period, and left early. His personal appearance was sloppy. He had virtually given himself early retirement, which his management then made formal.

Probably this man was frightened by the prospect of new management and the demands it might make on him or by the close examination it might make of his work. Perhaps there were other deeper reasons. The withdrawal was conspicuous, but the reasons were unclear. Much of sickness absenteeism, many accidents, apathy, turnover, and similar events may be viewed as forms of withdrawal. As such, they should call attention to the work area in which they occur, for symptoms reflect the existence of underlying problems.

As with other symptoms, withdrawal can occur because of unconscious conflicts that seem to mount with no apparent external pressure. Sometimes there are clues that a person is becoming increasingly restless, nervous, or withdrawn. But sometimes, too, the first indication of a problem is that the person fails to show up for work.

Sheldon Seeman seemed to be a friendly, intelligent man in his late twenties. When in public he was well dressed and polite. In private, he led an uneventful life and had few friends. He worked as a shipping clerk in a garment factory, a job which he handled to the satisfaction of his employer, except that there was no telling what morning he would fail to appear. For no apparent reason, he would complain to his landlady that he was not feeling well and would remain in bed. Sometimes weeks would go by before he went back to work. He just was not up to it, he would say. And then he would return to work as if he had never been away.

When a person begins to withdraw, it is important for others to make special efforts to maintain contact with him without being intrusive. In simple, everyday ways you can tell another person that you like him and you do not want to lose touch with him. Just the way you say "hello" is an important communication. If withdrawal usually results when a person finds relationships with others too painful and difficult, then you must resist the tendency to overwhelm him with interest, sympathy, and demands. It is enough to let the person know that you are interested and that you care about him. If he is pressured into joining the group or being more active, he will tend to withdraw even more. Casual but continued kindness, however, begins to rebuild bonds of trust, which the person can use to regain his ties outside himself whenever he is ready to do so.

CHRONIC REACTIONS

Like other reactions, withdrawal reactions can become chronic. A person may withdraw repeatedly from many different stress situations, functioning well between times, or he may withdraw and stay withdrawn, unable to remain at work. Extremely severe withdrawal, which involves loss of contact with reality, requires hospitalization.

One type of chronic withdrawal is that following painful shock, often seen in connection with occupational injuries or other sudden and frightening events. Such people act as if they have been hurt so severely that they dare not expose themselves again to possible hurt. Here is one example:

A thirty-six-year-old truck driver was involved in an accident in which his truck hit a car, killing one person and injuring two others. After the accident he began to complain of constant pain in his stomach, poor appetite, and frequent nausea. There was no physical basis for his symptoms, but his physician continued to treat him for his discomfort. Six months after the accident, he was able to return to work. He improved rapidly after he started working again. Five months later, however, a bus made a sharp turn in front of his truck, catching the front bumper of the truck in the rear fender of the bus. The driver was slightly shaken up, but otherwise unhurt. His former physical complaints returned. After a few months at home, most of his symptoms disappeared, but he still did not feel ready to return to work driving a truck. When nearly eight months had elapsed since the second accident, his company tried to get him to return to work in a job other than driving, but he made no effort to return.

In this kind of withdrawal, the ego remains intact. The person is able to think and act in a way that others can understand. It is understandable that a man could be so frightened of the possibility of having another accident and killing another person that he would not want to drive. It is more difficult to see why he would not take a nondriving job, but even at that, his behavior is not strange. Fear can cause a man to shrink in many ways, and the driver had reason to be afraid.

Some other forms of withdrawal are more baffling because people act in ways that we do not understand. In these reactions, the functioning of the ego is disrupted. Thinking and actions no longer seem rational, and the person loses some of his ability to test reality. He seems to be out of touch with what goes on around him.

A thirty-year-old sales supervisor for a food wholesaler became somewhat confused in his thinking and hesitant in his speech. He seemed emotionally flat, showing little interest in what went on around him. Gradually he withdrew from social contacts. His work level and efficiency decreased gradually to the point where he was unable to carry out the parts of his job that had been commonplace. His family reported that he had periods of confusion and suspiciousness. At times he laughed in a silly and inappropriate manner, and at other times his speech was wandering and illogical. He believed that the Fates had decreed that he should be mentally ill, and acting on their direction, he willingly entered a hospital.

In such a case, the ego is unable to control the person's behavior as it normally does. His feelings and thoughts seem unrelated to events outside himself and to each other. Unreal ideas and false perceptions, like hearing nonexistent voices, no longer seem strange to him. Such generalized disorganization of the personality always requires professional treatment and usually hospitalization.

Sometimes such behavior results from nonpsychological causes such as brain tumors, barbiturate poisoning, alcoholic intoxication, and severe upsets of the biochemical mechanisms of the body. Sometimes it occurs because of acute stress situations, as, for example, in states of severe shock. Sometimes it even occurs temporarily in experimental studies when all outside stimuli are cut off so that the person has no perceptions through his eyes, ears, sense of touch, or smell.

Many older men present a picture of withdrawal:

The supervisor of an engineering department is experienced in his field. Until about a year ago he did a satisfactory job. During the past year, those who worked with him found that he did not seem to comprehend problems or to grasp what had been going on around him. Now, if he is given a comprehensive written explanation of decisions that have been reached, he will still go off on a tangent or will start discussing and recommending matters that have already been carefully examined and discarded. Some of his most important cost estimates have been grossly in error. At the same time he is inclined to fancy himself as a negotiator, diplomat, and politician. He is reluctant to take responsibility for important matters that are under his own jurisdiction, but tends to edge over into other phases of the business, which are not truly his province. In addition, he has apparently provoked some minor personality irritations with top management and others.

The marked personality change within the period of a year indicates serious illness which requires thorough examination. The nature of this change is complex, but what the observer sees is mainly withdrawal: The person seems to be out of touch with the realities he once handled so well. It is as if he has detached himself from his surroundings. Withdrawal and loss of competence in a short period of time are common features of organic brain disease, something that could result from a tumor, from the degenerative process that accompanies aging, or from other changes in the brain. Sometimes, however, these changes take place more slowly. When these symptoms appear, diagnosis and treatment are clearly indicated.

These withdrawal reactions might better be described as catastrophic reactions because such a severe disturbance in the personality is indeed a psychological catastrophe. And if treatment is too long delayed, catastrophic reactions can become permanent states of withdrawal.

The layman who sees or hears about such bizarre behavior tends to assume that once the ego has been shattered, like Humpty Dumpty it can never be put back together again. "Once crazy, always crazy," is an old saw. Fortunately, unless the cause is organic, even people who are sick to this degree can recover; in good hospitals, more than 80 per cent of them do so.

Supervisors are naturally somewhat apprehensive about people who have had a severe illness and then return to work. They can be most helpful to the returning employee if they will simply accept him as just that, a returning employee, and treat him accordingly. Managers and supervisors who are concerned about former mental patients on the job should know that there are thousands of people in business, industry, education, the church, and government who have had such severe illnesses and who are doing their jobs normally. There are thousands more who have never been diagnosed or treated for mental illness, but who, if they were ever examined, would be diagnosed as chronically ill. Supportive and understanding supervisors, unaware of the fact that the employee is ill, nevertheless make it possible for him to do a good job. Thousands more could leave our mental hospitals and go back to work if jobs were available to them. There is ample evidence to indicate that many people who have been hospitalized for years can return to productive living.

MECHANISMS OF WITHDRAWAL

Denial is the major mechanism of withdrawal, and *projection* is usually a complementary mechanism. By withdrawing, the person is refusing to acknowledge the feelings that are disturbing him, or is simply avoiding the chore of coping with the outside world. He tries to make certain that his threatening impulses will not come into his consciousness. Projection, too, is a kind of denial, for this mechanism allows the person to attribute his feelings to someone else. For example, the "Fates," not the patient himself, decree that he should be mentally ill, and direct him to enter a hospital. His behavior, he feels, is not really his own, and someone else is responsible.

In severe withdrawal and catastrophic reactions, another phenomenon indicates the severity of the illness. This is the phenomenon of regression, or of retreating to an earlier stage in life. When people become ill, they may become childlike, and of course they require the care of others. When they become severely ill psychologically, when the ego is no longer able to maintain an equilibrium by means of adult behavior, it tries to do so by other means. Sometimes this results in reversion to a stage in life during which the person could cope more successfully with his problems, even if that stage was many years ago. For this reason, the behavior of seriously ill people often seems childish. Under no circumstances, however, should such a person be treated like a child, for such treatment would only prove to him that he is not capable of being an adult.

PERSONALITY TYPES

For some people, withdrawal is a style of life. They find themselves most comfortable away from others. Perhaps they prefer to walk alone in the woods rather than be at a noisy crowd at a ball game, or they choose quiet conversation with a friend rather than the excitement of a party. Sometimes they are creative people who need to be by themselves to think or create. Sometimes they are just "loners" without important attachments. Some people move frequently from one place to another, establishing no ties anywhere; others can stay in the same place for years and hardly be known to those who see them every day.

There is a common myth that those who prefer to be by themselves are peculiar. Certainly their behavior is different from that of the majority in a society that places a high value on being sociable and that makes them seem odd to others. Some are lonely, "different" personalities who want desperately to associate freely with others, but who either do not know how to do so or do not dare to do so. Some are afraid of being hurt; some have been hurt too much.

These, however, are the people who can do the lonely jobs that a society requires. Even more important are the perspectives and innovations they bring. Poets, scientists, inventors, social critics, all have to use their own thoughts as raw material. To do that, they have to be somewhat distant from others. They have to step back and look at what goes on, something they could not do if they were deeply en-meshed in the process.

Here is how such a man looks on the job, and the problems he poses, as described by one of his colleagues:

I have known Larry Bell for ten years. He was an ex-cellent student, I am told, and graduated from engineer-ing school with honors. He was also a good athlete. In manner he is friendly but very shy. He prefers to work alone, and works long hours for weeks at a time, turning out prodigious amounts of work. He is a thoroughly sound engineer and a brilliant analyst of engineering problems. He is probably the single most valuable em-ployee in our organization.

When I joined this organization, I was assigned as his assistant. Difficulties became apparent when I tried to learn the outline of my assignment, basic policies, the source of basic data necessary, and to obtain necessary checking, correction, and direction. I was treated cour-teously, a direct question would be answered, but nothing whatever was volunteered or expanded.

After two years my assignment was changed. We were required to work together as a team on some as-signments, frequently in consultation, and on joint solutions of major problems. Results under this arrange-ment were similar. Any direct question would be an-swered in a friendly manner, but nothing was added or volunteered. Any scheme that he might be working on would not be mentioned until it was on paper and ap-proved by higher authority. By the same token, schemes I suggested or proposed would be listened to, but in most cases he would take no further action on carrying them forward, even when they became the eventual solutions to the problems. At the same time, it should be noted that this was not the usual case of jealousy or interoffice rivalry. Relations remained entirely amicable, but the work, in my opinion, suffered from the lack of interplay of ideas and joint participation.

Now I have a higher position than he, but the problem remains. He is affable and, when directed by higher authority, will produce the minimum information requested. It is still not possible to discuss plans, organization, or operations on any kind of exploratory basis, or to come to any particular conclusion except in conference with the boss himself.

How should I manage to work concurrently with him? How do I get him to trust himself—and me—sufficiently to discuss futures, possibilities, and potentialities?

The most frequent mistake made with such people is to urge them to be more sociable. This usually follows the discovery that the shy, quiet person on the edge of the group has something useful to offer, or that he really is human after all. Since his style of life is to shun the spotlight and to avoid closeness to others, such pressure makes him shrink even more. As in so many other situations, a consistently warm, friendly, interested attitude, which remains casual, shows such a person that you are interested in him, and will be glad to talk with him whenever he wishes. This permits him the initiative, when he can lower his defenses sufficiently to take a chance.

It is easy to overlook such people, to think that they do not need recognition and praise. Since they tend to be silent in meetings, their contributions are often lost unless a discerning chairman holds off the more talkative participants to give them an opportunity. Sometimes, even then, they cannot say what they have to offer, which might be obtained in private conference afterward.

Having discovered the capabilities of a talented but withdrawn person, an executive may wish to push him into positions of greater responsibility. But these positions often require interaction with others, which puts such a person at a disadvantage. If he cannot withdraw, he may then actively push others away. His superiors then become angry with him and repeatedly urge him to behave otherwise, to no avail:

A forty-year-old cost analyst who heads a sizeable department is highly intelligent and technically well qualified. He is articulate and an incisive thinker. He talks down to his people and makes them feel as though they know nothing and he knows it all. He will go into great detail to explain background and facts, emphasizing further the "know it all" impression. There are times when it appears that he delights in making himself offensive. People tend to avoid him except when necessary. Considering that he can make a contribution and is sound in his thinking, the company loses out when colleagues and subordinates do not turn to him. The effect of his behavior has been pointed out to him, and he has been told that his manner inhibits his advancement. But he apparently does not want to change. He seems not to be interested in social position or in the material things in life, and he does not want to take on more responsibility.

Such a problem perhaps could have been avoided by observing the man's relations with others in his previous jobs and by talking over the demands of the new job. This man might well have been far more important to his organization in a consultation or individual staff role than in a situation requiring constant and close interrelationships with others. A wise supervisor might help his co-workers to understand this man's efforts to keep them away so that they would not be frightened off. The boss should not keep up frontal assault efforts to rescue the man from himself.

CHAPTER 8

Hostility Reactions

IF FLIGHT IS THE MODE OF DEFENSE IMPLICIT IN WITHDRAWAL reactions, then fight is clearly the mode of defense in hostility reactions. Hostility reactions, of all the defensive maneuvers, are most evident to other people. In hostility reactions, anger bursts through the controls of the ego with sometimes devastating results, and always with apparent justification in the eyes of the person who is aggressive. He is quite certain that he has every right to feel that way and to act on his feelings.

Hostility reactions are probably the most uncomfortable and the most difficult reactions to cope with. The hostile person induces fear and anger in others. Sometimes they would just as soon leave him alone. At other times, their impulse is to return anger for anger. When either fear or anger are induced in the other person, his own defenses are put into play. Rising anger, particularly, calls for strong controls to prevent aggressive outbursts. When a man's anger rises in response to someone else's, his controls are threatened. Furthermore, he may have guilt feelings because of his aggressive impulses. Such feelings may keep him from acting forthrightly to deal with the problem. In short, in hostility reactions, you have to deal not only with the angry person but with yourself and your own controls as well. Your own mounting anger may cause you to let yourself be a target for the hostile person, or it may cause you to react impulsively.

Hostility reactions vary in style: (1) Some people seem to lie in wait. They may get along very well with another person until the other person "crosses them," however unwittingly. Then they attack him for violating their trust and reject him out of hand. (2) Some are perennially angry, lashing out at others who can never live up to their ideals, standards, values, or expectations. With caustic criticism, they wield a whip of words on all that goes on around them, for the imperfections of human beings give them constant fodder for explosion. (3) Some see danger threatening them on many sides. Some one or some group is out "to get" them, or to get what they stand for. The keynote of this behavior is the belief that others are plotting, and therefore one is justified in attacking the plotters.

The common theme is the inability to trust others and the effort to suppress the hurtful actions of others. A parallel theme is the extreme difficulty in accepting the possibility that one may be wrong. Together, these traits make for a guarded readiness to defend and attack. They are evident in this fairly typical case:

A thirty-four-year-old engraver was seen in a company medical department when he complained of a headache and, vaguely, of stomach distress. In six years with the company, he had been to the medical department thirty-six times, chiefly for headaches and vague intestinal complaints. He had been working in his present department three years and previously had worked in two other departments. The physician began to look more carefully into his history of frequent illness. While the patient was being interviewed, he was tense and tearful; he spoke in a loud tone of voice and swore several times. He said that since he had been transferred to his present department, he had the feeling that his fellow workers and his supervisor were against him and no one seemed to appreciate his abilities. He admitted to being "hot headed" and to speaking out of turn at times. He had been a union officer, but gave up his position because the other officers criticized him. Recently he had been denied a raise, so he had taken a complaint through the grievance procedure. He had also requested that he be allowed to work on certain equipment, a request that had also been denied. Because of these many evidences of "mistreatment," he had requested an appointment with the plant manager to discuss his problems.

When the doctor checked with the man's supervisor, the latter rounded out the picture like this. It was true that some of the men teased the engraver a great deal. He obtained the job he had because no one else wanted it. He was known throughout the plant as a "loud-mouth." He always seemed to feel that he could do a job better than anyone else and would blame others for tinkering with his work when they had not done so. He resented anyone who tried to help him, and soon people stopped trying to help him, and some ceased speaking to him. As a matter of fact, his work was below average, and at times some of it had to be discarded. He had been told of the poor quality of his work, but it did not improve. It was true that he had been a union officer, but not that he had quit of his own volition. He had raised so many false issues for grievances that the other officers asked him to resign.

He had quit his previous job to go into a small business for himself. He sold that business because the hours were too long, but his previous employer had not wanted him back because he had quit without notice and could not get along with his supervisors.

ACUTE REACTIONS

Acute hostility reactions may occur in response to external events for which the person senses that he may be responsible, blamed, or criticized. Unable to face his superego with his possible shortcomings, he denies his own part in the events by attributing the fault to others. This is what the engraver in the preceding example did.

Putting the blame on others is a commonplace reaction. When, for example, employees in a plant become unionized, the employer sometimes attributes that behavior to "outside agitators" who "stirred them up." He fails to recognize what he himself may have done to precipitate this action, which would be an examination of how he handles his own aggressions. By denying his own aggressions, he can then feel righteously indignant that his employees are angry at him. Here is a not unusual situation:

A plant manager in a heavy industry plant is tightly governed by controls from his central office. Each step of the production process is laid out for him. Statistical reports are a feature of his everyday work life. He has little flexibility of operation. In turn, he expects his employees to do as they are told and to produce a fair day's work for a fair wage. His assumption is that his employees are in the plant only to sell their services for which he pays them. He does not expect them to like what they do or to get any gratification from it. He believes they should understand management's production goals and meet them in order to provide a return for the stockholders. He cannot understand why the employees are less than enthusiastic, particularly since the company gives them what the management considers to be good fringe benefits. He does not acknowledge that the benefits were won after bitter battles in labor negotiations. He cannot understand either why the employees "always want more" and he decides that they are trying to gain the upper hand over the company—even trying to destroy the company. Whenever things go wrong, whether criticism from higher management or some difficulty in the plant, he reacts by criticizing the employees and by trying to control them more tightly. This behavior does not solve his problems, for the anger of the men is then displaced onto the work process. The more the boss fumes, the more the men laugh at him behind his back and the more the work process is disrupted. When the pressure is off him, the aggression in his banter with the men becomes more veiled, as if he were trying to soften his angry verbal jabs at them.

An acute hostility reaction can occur when external events stimulate internal impulses that the person is already having difficulty controlling. Seeing other people do what one unconsciously wants to do is one example. There are people who go to great lengths to control their own sexual impulses by avoiding any suggestion of sexual matters. For them, the world is sexless. When such a person is directly faced with sexual stimuli that he cannot avoid, such as a suggestive motion picture or a dirty joke, he may well become extremely angry.

For other people the touchy subject may be their race or

religion. For still others it may be politics or a handicap of some sort. Angry overreaction tells us that the person has strong feelings about the particular subject which are not well controlled. Some men, without knowing why, are aroused to anger because their children indulge in behavior that has been forbidden to them. Others become angry when subordinates, not having the same rigid superegos, laugh and joke freely on the job.

Acute reactions also occur from mounting internal conflict. For reasons unknown to both the person who has the reaction and those who observe it, a person may live with mounting tension from day to day. Suddenly, as if he can tolerate the tension no longer, he explodes in anger. Then, having discharged his hostility, he is reasonably calm for a period of time. This behavior puzzles everyone concerned and makes others wary because they do not know at what point they may be attacked.

Leo Handy, in his mid-forties, is a creative advertising writer and a producer of advertising films. He is regarded as talented but temperamental. He is completely intolerant of anyone who does not match his mental acuity. Despite his talent, he does not deliver as well or as consistently as he should because his emotions get in the way. Sometimes he writes brilliantly and produces prize-winning copy and films. Sometimes he is so slow that it seems as if he will not be finished on time. Others cannot help him because he is never satisfied with their efforts.

For a while, Handy complains constantly about being oppressed by the incompetence of clients, superiors, and subordinates. Then, in turn, he can be good hearted and thoughtful of others. He responds hungrily to praise and seeks it out if it is not volunteered.

He ridicules his boss' suggestions, but then he will work on the boss' ideas half-heartedly and with much complaint. When he is not in an angry mood, his work improves, but his relaxed phases do not last long. Soon he is complying with suggestions only because, in his own mind, he is tolerant and willing to bend.

Hostility reactions, reflecting the loss of a person's control over his aggressions, require that help from others which will reinforce the ego's controls. Help can proceed in three stages: (1) Diminish the defensiveness that produced the reaction. You may temporarily have to absorb the hostility without becoming frightened or angry yourself, so that the angry person need not become more defensive. (2) Ease the self-criticism which may follow the hostility reaction so that guilt will not produce more hostility. You may indicate to the person, perhaps by your own calmness, that it is not unusual for a person to lose control of his temper. As long as he does not hurt anyone else, no damage is done. When you do not become angry in turn, it shows that you understand there is a reason for the hostility reaction. By not withdrawing, you indicate that you still hold the angry person in esteem. Such communication of understanding and respect supports the ego in re-establishing its controls. (3) Reinforce the controls by refusing to permit the repetition of the behavior. You have not rejected the person for losing control of himself temporarily. Rather you have supported him in his difficulty. This does not mean, however, that as his supervisor, colleague, subordinate, or friend you must let yourself be the target for his hostility again and again. In fact, you cannot permit him to attack you or others repeatedly. If he cannot help feeling angry, then he must work out a way to handle his anger less destructively. If this is impossible, then he needs professional help, and he may have to leave the job until he acquires some control.

Here is the way these principles were applied in a management training conference:

One of the participants in a training program became angry with the training staff. As each lecturer and discussion leader raised issues about the management of people, the participant interrupted and challenged the speaker out of proportion to ordinary animated discussion. The other participants soon began to quarrel with him and the staff were ready to send him home. When it was pointed out to the staff that they might inadvertently be attacking him at his most vulnerable spot, his inability to relate himself well to his subordinates, they contained their anger. Then, instead of attacking him in return and letting others attack him, they gave due recognition to the points he raised as being important considerations. Rather than permitting him to interrupt them constantly, they asked him to hold his questions until the appropriate time for questions and discussion. They interwove replies to some of the concerns he had already expressed, by referring to his points when it was appropriate to do so.

As the man felt less threatened, he attacked less. Finally, at one point, he blurted out with almost painful embarrassment that he did not want to manage people. He did not know how to do so, he said, and he would rather do his own specialized work by himself. To this, the discussion leader replied that not everyone did want to be a manager, and certainly not everyone had the interests and the skills to do so. A man did not have to feel inadequate just because he did not want to be a manager. Many different kinds of skills were needed in a business, and he had other skills which were extremely important to his company.

The man's frank statement of his feelings indicated that he felt secure enough in the group to speak freely about his discomfort when he was being asked to do something he could not do. When the rest of the group understood the reason for his anger, they stopped attacking him. Instead, they came to his support. They sought him out for conversation, made certain that he was invited to their informal bull sessions, and in other ways brought him into the group. He presented no problem for the rest of the training program.

CHRONIC REACTIONS

When hostility becomes a chronic phenomenon, it tends to be diffuse. The person first sees many different people and groups as threatening. Gradually, his fear tends to be focused on some people or a few groups. He then directs his attack to them. This is the mechanism behind most prejudice and scapegoating. It should be obvious that a person who is constantly hostile because he is seeing hostility where none exists, is sick and needs professional treatment. No amount of procrastination or persuasion will alter his behavior. Here is a case in point:

An executive had been with his firm twenty-five years, having started from the bottom when he was twenty-five years old. He had always been a conscientious worker. When he began to supervise others, he considered everyday business problems to be personal. If an employee was disobedient or disloyal, he thought the

man was being disloyal to him personally. He thought of
his subordinates as "my men," but his use of the phrase
did not mean the same as it might for someone else. He
could not distinguish between his problem and the company's, between his temporary "possession" of the men
to do a piece of work and "owning" them. It was as if
they were part of him. Soon there were reports of his
"lording it over" the men. He would reprimand them
in an angry, bellowing voice, becoming very excited in
the process. Sometimes he would call them down in
front of other people. He then began to behave in the
same way with office personnel with whom he had been
associated amicably for years. Sometimes he would
storm into a department, single out a culprit, and tear
into his victim unmercifully, even to the point of swear-
ing at him.

His colleagues took this for a while, explaining away
his behavior by saying that he did not mean it. He was
just blowing off steam they said, and basically he was a
good person. They recognized that he was usually right
about the matters he picked on, and they told themselves that he really had the interests of the company at
heart.

His high position in the firm seems to have given him
a "big shot complex," as his colleagues see it. He alone
can make decisions and others had better not cross him,
or even act on their own, if what they are doing in any
way affects his department. Since there is a good deal
of overlap of activities, this manner presents a constant
problem. He complains about the inefficiency of key
people. He contends that he is overworked, but this
apparently is a result of his inability to delegate.

Evidently this man overcontrolled his hostile impulses until he reached a point in the executive hierarchy where he felt he did not have to fear anyone above him. Then he really let go, and the underlying personality pattern of rigidity and hostility was exposed.

Demands that the person control his behavior usually result only in temporary and poorly sustained improvement. When the reaction becomes a severe one, suspiciousness and distance from other people increases to the point of irrationality. The person expects the worst from other people and is constantly on guard against them. Sometimes he develops an organized system of ideas of persecution, building isolated events into a "logical" story which he firmly believes. Sometimes also he is litigious, constantly engaged in lawsuits to get "his rights." In the most severe cases, the person's false beliefs require that he be hospitalized.

A middle-aged woman was reported to be causing dissension in her department. Investigation disclosed that she had frequently implied or directly accused her supervisor of letting many other people in the department get by without doing much work, and of being partial to some employees. She said that the supervisor made fun of her and that she was going to get a governmental agency after him, which incidentally she did. She had also told others in the department that the supervisor had been "getting fresh" with her and that he was involved with one of the other women who worked in the department. Investigation proved her allegations to be untrue.

During medical examination she was defensive and evasive. For a while she carefully avoided any reference to her supervisor, and then said that something was going on in the department and that her repeated requests for transfers had been denied. (She had in fact been transferred a number of times before coming to the present department.) She then repeated her accusations that the supervisor had tried to become familiar with her. When she was referred for treatment, she refused to be treated, saying that the only reason she was in the psychiatrist's office was because the company physician had sent her there.

MECHANISMS OF HOSTILITY REACTIONS

The major mechanism of hostility reactions is *projection*. Hostile people are angry people. Their hostility is unacceptable to their own superegos, so they repress it. But repressing the hostility only makes it unconscious; it does not disappear. Instead, it presses the ego for expression. For some people, the only solution is to release the hostility, but what if this is forbidden by the superego? One way is to pacify the superego. It is justifiable for these people to be angry with someone else if that person is hostile to them. The solution is simple, expedient, and unconscious: Believe the other person to be hostile; then you can vent your hostility on him with no complaint from the superego.

So, hostile people overuse projection and rationalization. It takes a lot of rationalization to make the world seem hostile. And if rationalizing does not work well enough to support projection, there is always the very effective avenue of provoking people to anger. Most people will soon respond to provocation and attack the person who makes himself a target. Then he can truthfully say people hate him, reject him, and even punish him. By the time this occurs, it is almost impossible to tell who is the victim and who is the aggressor. Only the repetition of this problem shows that it is of the man's own making. Unfortunately, by the time enough repetition has occurred for someone to be aware of it and take action, the person involved has usually been in the organization long enough for the organization to feel obligated to him. The obligation becomes even more pressing when it becomes apparent that some people have indeed treated him shabbily after he has provoked them. The layman rarely observes the provocation. Indeed, he finds it difficult to believe that people would provoke others to attack them. He therefore is reluctant to take action against an employee who has been having such a hard time of it. Besides, the employee's hostility frightens him and thereby increases his reluctance to act. Take this example, for instance:

Ralph's job is to set up the work for an assembly line. He has been doing this job for years, and each year he complains to the plant superintendent that his foreman treats him badly. Ralph says his foreman will pay attention to him only when he complains, but will not answer his complaints or talk about anything with him.

Bill, the foreman, says Ralph will take whatever he says, turn it around, and report it to someone else in entirely different fashion so as to make an issue out of it. Ralph is excitable and talks so fast that he will not give Bill a chance to respond to whatever questions Ralph asks him.

Ralph is limited in his capacity. He feels overloaded if Bill asks him to be responsible for several things on his job, although the job requires it. Ralph does not refuse to do a job when it is assigned, but he thinks he is being overworked no matter what the assignment may be. He feels Bill is discriminating against him if he does not get complete details about all that is going on in the department, even if it has nothing to do with his job.

Ralph complains that the foreman will not take his requests to the general foreman. The general foreman says the foreman is usually too busy to come running with requests as they are made. Ralph feels all his questions should be handled like crises, with immediate favorable responses. Furthermore, he misinterprets what is said to him as being hostile and rejecting. The superintendent believes Ralph is shrewd and knows just how far he can go without being fired. He needles people who work with him, but is on his best behavior in front of superiors.

PERSONALITY TYPES

If the ego has such difficulty with aggression that it must distort reality to handle it, then the ego must be having difficulty maintaining its defenses. The more pressure on the defenses, the less flexible the ego is likely to be. As a result, those who characteristically exhibit hostility reactions are likely to be rigid in their thinking. Perceiving the outside world as hostile, they will be hyperalert to threats and therefore attentive to detail. Such people give such exquisite attention to the tiny nuances of details and relationships that they remind one of an Indian scout in enemy country.

If, sensing their own hostility, they need to be rigid to control it, then others who are presumed to be hostile need to be controlled too. These people therefore seek power or control over others. With power, they are defensively aloof and somewhat pretentious in their relationships with others. They exude the impression that they are somehow better than others.

Thus we have the picture of an alert, highly organized,

dominating person who tends to operate by himself. He is likely to be intelligent and to pursue power. He gravitates therefore to leadership positions. Often he builds great organizations, but cannot sustain them. (Henry Ford, a case in point, was so suspicious that he never could permit others to have power in his organization.) Often he leads a cause to victory or near-victory, only to turn on his friends when there was no longer an outside enemy. He knows no compromise, for his rigidity makes him see black and white, right and wrong, we or they. He quickly becomes obsolete, for the world changes and he does not.

This description characterizes many of the business leaders of a generation ago and the barons of business before that. It characterizes also some of our leading politicians. Hitler and Stalin were extreme examples of this type. Such a personality type inevitably presents certain on-the-job problems, as in this case:

Edwin Sands is in his middle forties and presently holds a very important position as assistant comptroller in his company. He is highly ambitious to advance, and from all standpoints except his relations with people, has no foreseeable limitation on his capacity to do so. He has a keen, sharp, analytic mind. He is recognized for his technical grasp and proficiency. He is one of the hardest working, most aggressive men in the company. He is personally very attractive and likable. Casual relations with him create the impression that here is a man of really outstanding potential. He is well read and versed on many of the problems of top management and on good administrative methods. Yet in day-to-day dealings, he is so assertive and so determined in what he believes that he alienates his associates. They feel he is so "hell bent" in insisting on his views that he is oblivious to theirs, and he walks "rough shod" over their opinions and feelings. They acknowledge his competence, but want no part of him in a more responsible position on the management team. His subordinates, at least in the past, have also been quite unhappy, and a number have indicated they would not like to work for him again.

This has been discussed frankly with him by his present boss. If his previous superiors had ever done so, they made little impression on him because he has no recollection of such a discussion.

He is a sincere and conscientious person who takes what is said seriously, but since he is so insensitive to the fact that others are reacting negatively to him, it is also hard for him to understand why or what he must do to overcome it. He has responded affirmatively to the suggestion of spending some time with a business counselor, with the objective of helping him to understand himself better, to see better how he appears to others, and to help him do something about it. This was suggested because it is expected that his positiveness and compulsive need to be right is deep-seated and goes back to experiences that can best be dealt with by someone with professional training. In addition, by the company paying the fee and having him appraise the value of this counselor for further use by the company, he knows that the company continues its confidence and belief in him. At the same time, the company is communicating that he is hurting himself by his methods, and can be a better man if he changes. He wants to correct this deficiency and progress in the company, but fears that so much prejudice has built up against him that he can never fully overcome it.

Without intensive treatment, this man is not going to change significantly. His company will not make a sensitive, supportive leader out of him. He would, however, be just the man for starting a crash program or rescuing a failing company, where the feelings of others would be sacrificed to the emergency task. An employer should be alert to the possible unrealistic expectations he may have of subordinates like this.

In mild form, personality traits like these can be put to good use. Certainly we need people who want to lead, for we need leaders in many different institutions, even though there are shortcomings to their leadership. We need people with initiative and drive to build organizations and to move causes. We need people who have tendencies to martyrdom, whose sacrifice brings about necessary social change.

At a simpler level, we need people who want to control others—people who make the law and those who enforce it. Those who enforce it tend to be more direct in their aggressions than those who make it, so there is always danger when the enforcers become the lawmakers. It is interesting to note that the strongest opponents of outlawing capital punishment are the police chiefs.

We also need alert people as inspectors, accountants, lawyers, medical diagnosticians. In short, there are many ways to make effective use of people whose hostility is a conspicuous part of their personalities. But it must be clear that these people will not be noted for their good human relations.

CHAPTER 9

Bodily Reactions

ALTHOUGH THE MIND AND THE BODY ARE A UNIFIED WHOLE, IT is important to make an artificial distinction between them in order to study these different facets of the person more easily. Psychological stress engenders physiological stress, and vice versa. There are physical symptoms in every emotional illness. In some emotional illnesses, however, physical symptoms are the most conspicuous evidences of stress and the major mode for coping with the stress.

Physical symptoms in parts of the body over which the person usually has control, such as arms and legs, were mentioned in Chapter 5. Loss of voluntary control over limbs became the symptom. This chapter will examine psychologically induced symptoms in body organs over which the person has no voluntary control.

Bodily symptoms tend to occur when two things happen: (1) When the ego has to cope with a new stress at a time when it is already grappling with one and it does not have quite enough energy to fend off the new threat. The common cold is a good example. The germs of the common cold are always with us. They seem to produce symptoms only when

112

a person's resistance is lowered. It can be lowered for physical reasons or because the ego is diverting so much energy to psychological problems. (2) When the emergency alarm mechanism, anxiety, activates defensive maneuvers again and again, ultimately bringing about physiological wear and tear. This happens particularly, as was discussed in Chapter 4, when the ego tries to contain impulses. Relatively simple stress situations upset the digestive system or result in headaches or other minor illnesses. Worry often results in physical fatigue. More severe or repetitive stress produces actual damage to the systems involved.

ACUTE REACTIONS

External events often precipitate diffuse bodily reactions. The coincidence of the event with the reaction makes the relationship between them apparent, particularly when the reaction disappears after circumstances change. The diffuse quality of the reaction indicates a generalized attempt of the ego to deal with threat.

A middle-management executive was making good progress through the ranks of a railroad company. He was promoted to a divisional staff job, having had a good work record with regular promotions and salary increases. He then began to have physical symptoms: stomach pain, bloating, vomiting, headache, backache, and indigestion. These he reported to his family physician, together with the feeling that he was not competent to handle his new responsibilities. He had been quite content with his previous post, which he handled without difficulty. However, he did not dare to ask for a demotion because to do so would be to admit failure and to be looked down upon by his superiors. He had not told his superiors of his symptoms. His physician told him he would have to give up his new job. He was then able to report to his superiors that, for health reasons, he was unable to assume the heavier responsibilities. When he was reassigned, his symptoms disappeared.

In this case, external events threatened to overwhelm the ego. The man felt he could not cope with his responsibilities. Other external events stimulate impulses that threaten to overwhelm the ego from the inside:

A newly appointed sales manager increased the sales for his company by concentrating heavily on specialty items which incidentally, had a higher profit margin than standard items. As a result, he contributed significantly to profitability and became the favorite of the president. His success was at the expense of the production manager, who was given no new help or equipment to produce the increased volume. The new volume was also harder to produce because it was in short runs requiring considerable downtime to readjust the machines and quality control was more difficult to maintain. These factors slowed production and, in turn, deliveries. As a result, the sales manager was constantly pressing the production manager. The production manager was already resentful for having lost his favored position with the president. He became more so with increasing pressure from the sales manager. One day the sales manager stomped out onto the production floor and berated the production manager publicly. The production manager, who up to this point had controlled his temper relatively well, exploded. After giving vent to a number of impulsively chosen, highly colorful phrases, he ordered the sales manager off the floor. Thereupon he ran for the men's room where he threw up.

In this situation, aggressive impulses came much too close to the surface for the production manager. He was sickened by the thought that, "I could have murdered the so-and-so." Actually, he would not have murdered the sales manager, but when he felt himself ready to strike the sales manager, it was literally possible for him to murder in anger. The ego could not tolerate that possibility and mobilized its defenses, upsetting the digestive system.

Medical diagnosis should be routine for all physical symptoms. Executive diagnosis of the work situation should also be routine. Often there are no evident external events that precipitate symptoms. The less evident the precipitating events, the greater the indication that the stress arises from unconscious conflict. Where the external events are apparent, you can do something about changing them. Where they are not apparent, of course, you cannot know the precipitants of the problem. In such instances, professional help is required. This case is a good example:

Eric Zale joined his company six years ago as personnel director. He had done academic graduate work and had had business experience with other companies. He came to a job that was well defined. He was responsible for all personnel practices, though much of his responsibility would be carried out through line supervisors. He was responsible also for industrial relations, which included union negotiations, for liaison with employee social groups, and for community relations. He was also to take an active part in executive decision making.

These responsibilities were not overwhelming because two predecessors had carried them out successfully over a ten-year period.

From the beginning, Zale relished the executive decision-making group and avoided relating himself to any community organization. Union relations took little time because of long-standing good labor relations. He thus spent most of his time on personnel practices and liaison with employee social groups.

Every year at annual appraisal time, he reported that he was overworked, that his health was suffering, and that he needed to have his responsibilities trimmed. Since he was highly regarded as a person and he was not physically rugged, his requests were granted. This pattern was not recognized as it progressed, but after four years his job had been narrowed to personnel practices and executive decision making. The other responsibilities had been ignored or shifted to other persons. Later in that year, he asked for an assistant to help carry the personnel load, and that request also was granted.

About the same time, his colleagues became aware that Zale had come to talk almost like a medical doctor, that he was chronically ill and under the treatment of a variety of physicians, and that he was constantly taking medicine. His colleagues found this irritating or joked about it, depending on how it interfered with their work—until he collapsed into unconsciousness during a staff meeting. Then it was discovered that he was the patient of seven different physicians, none of whom knew he was being treated by any of the others, and that he was taking daily ten times the prescribed dosage of pain-relieving medicine.

At company expense, he was referred to a university hospital for examination. The examining physician reported there was no organic cause for his complaints, but that his perception and ability to concentrate were severely limited. Because of this and his addiction to his medication, he then had to be hospitalized.

CHRONIC REACTIONS

When repetitive stress results from unconscious conflicts, the stress tends to be specific. That is, there is a repetitive struggle with the same conflict. The bodily reaction also becomes chronic. The anxiety is "bound" to that symptom. The symptom often reflects the nature of the conflict. What happens with ulcers is a good example.

As was indicated in Chapter 1, because of the long period during which children are dependent on their parents, particularly in Western cultures, everyone struggles with the conflict between his wishes to be dependent and cared for, and his desire to become a self-sufficient adult. This is essentially an id-superego conflict. For some it is a more difficult conflict than for others, and it tends to become even more difficult when that person has to assume responsibility for other people. He is required to accept someone else's dependence when he has not been able to satisfy his own dependency needs.

When people are under psychological stress, it is not surprising that primitive reactions are awakened. Under stress, a person struggling with a dependency problem will unconsciously wish to be protected and cared for as he once was in the arms of his mother. The repressed memories of that security and pleasure keep trying to enter consciousness. The ego, responding to the superego, forbids such thoughts

—a man must be a man and stand on his own. But the memories of pleasure and protection continue to exist and exert a force on the ego.

Being loved and being fed were simultaneous experiences in infancy. When the primitive wish to be loved is stimulated under stress, so is the primitive wish to be fed. The wish to be fed, in turn, stimulates physical activity related to eating. The stomach acts as if it were going to receive food and increases its flow of digestive juices. The excess of digestive juices wears away the stomach lining and produces an ulcer.

The ulcer may be treated medically or surgically or psychologically or by a combination of these. Every bodily reaction to psychological stress always requires medical treatment together with psychological treatment. If the conflict is not resolved, the ulcer is likely to recur in acute periods of stress, which often happens when treatment is limited to the physical symptom itself.

Similar reactions occur in other parts of the body. Some people have difficulty breathing during stress periods, experiencing such symptoms as shortness of breath or asthma. "Irritable bowel" or mucous colitis is a very common bodily reaction to psychological tension. Others have skin lesions and still others have a wide range of symptoms. They seem to respond to almost all stress with some part of their bodies. That is why a small percentage of employees make up a large part of the case load in any medical department.

Extended studies of more than 3,400 actively employed men and women, in some cases over a 35-year period of employment, have been done in the New York Telephone Company. Twenty-five per cent of these employees accounted for more than half of all episodes of disability, approximately two-thirds of all days of disability, and a similar proportion of the cost of sickness. The same group had more different kinds of sicknesses than did the others, more disturbances of mood and behavior, and were more frequently involved in administrative difficulties. "Attention to an unsatisfactory life situation may be more important than any other aspect of treatment," the reporting physicians conclude.[3]

Almost any physical symptom can be precipitated by psychological stress, but this is not to say that all physical symptoms are psychological in origin. There is, furthermore, not a one-to-one correlation between a particular kind of stress and a particular symptom. There is fairly common agreement among psychiatrists about the precipitants of ulcer. Peptic ulcers occur more frequently in first-level supervisors, where others are more clearly and directly dependent upon the supervisors, than either at the line level or in higher levels.[4]

One kind of stress, which appears to be related to coronary disease, is excessive responsibility for the control and direction of one's own behavior.[5] This kind of stress in turn is a product of strong superego. Those who have had coronaries often say that they do not act without thinking and that they rarely "sit and do nothing." They also compete with authority figures and have more fear of authority figures than noncoronaries. Consequently, they do not achieve occupationally as well as noncoronaries (a fact supported by studies of Dupont executives[6]). The authors of this study observe, "It would appear that coronaries are restless and anxious if they do not compete, and unsuccessful and inadequate when they do compete."

Allowing for the fact that this is a statistical study that deals in proportions and probabilities, and therefore it cannot be said specifically of each coronary victim that he has this specific psychological conflict, coronary illness on the whole seems to relate to difficulties in dealing with unconscious hostility toward the father. But this is not the only issue. In the study just summarized, there were twice as many Protestants as Catholics among the coronaries, and a preponderance of middle-class over lower-class men, again suggesting that those who can comfortably lean on authority are less likely to have coronaries. Diet, smoking, and other factors are also related to coronary disease.

The important point, as far as you are concerned, is not that there appear to be significant correlations between certain stresses and bodily reactions, but that bodily reactions are frequently symptoms of psychological stress. You are not going to treat the bodily illness, physical or psychological. You can, however, be aware of the possibility of psychological factors in the illness, and you can carefully review the work situation for its contribution to undue stress as well as refer the person to the proper sources of help. You might also be alert to your own bodily reactions and the events that seem to precipitate them.

Even with chronic reactions, there is something the layman can do in many situations. You can often relieve the pressure that precipitates a symptom by sizing the situation accurately and introducing counterforces that diminish the threat. Here is an example:

A long-time employee had risen to an important technical job by means of self-training and experience. He had a more successful older brother who owned his own business. This technician preferred to be alone much of the time, often working irregular hours at night on technical problems. He got along reasonably well until a new college-trained technician was added to the staff. The older man became apprehensive because he did not have a college degree and his apprehension, with its accompanying hostility, led to projection. He came to feel that the other man was "out to get him," even to hurt him physically. No amount of reassurance from his superiors relieved his stress. He became increasingly upset and developed skin lesions all over his body. Fortunately, the man's wife sought the help of the company physician. The physician advised her to reassure him that his job was not threatened and to increase her attention and psychological support. He advised the boss to continue his reassurance. In effect, the wife was to mother him more and the man's superior was to be the supportive but realistic father. The rivalry situation, with its roots deep in the man's childhood, would not be resolved without professional help. But with the combined support of his wife, a dermatologist, the company physician and his boss, the skin condition cleared up and he was able to return to his work.

The superior helped specifically by being part of a team on a job he could not do alone. While the wife gave affection, the superior provided realistic support—stressing the fact that the man would not be demoted or lose his job. Thus two important counterforces were injected into the situation to help the ego maintain an equilibrium. In this case, the counterforce helped relieve a specific symptom. In other cases, it may be added help in getting a job done or reaching a decision, or even defining exactly what is to be done. In any event, a counterforce is some specific action that communicates to the person that he is not being left alone with his problems.

REPRESSION AS THE BASIS FOR THE SYMPTOM

As has been explained, most psychosomatic symptoms occur because the ego seems to have no satisfactory way of discharging the mounting pressure of the impulse. What occurs in the human body is much like what occurs in any other closed system when internal pressure mounts. Parts within the system are subject to unusual wear, and external surfaces give way at various points. The major mechanism for containing the impulses is repression. As a result, the person is usually unaware of any connection between his physical symptom and its psychological origins. When the relationship becomes clear, as in some forms of treatment, the symptom usually disappears, and more satisfactory ways of dealing with the problem take its place.

PERSONALITY TYPES

If a bodily symptom pattern becomes established in the personality as a routine way of coping with stress, then it becomes a crippling, inefficient, high-cost defense. A man takes out his problems on his own body rather than finding some more appropriate and effective solution for them. When bodily symptoms become characteristic modes of adaptation, they tend to occur with fair regularity in certain kinds of people. Ulcers, which are related to dependent wishes, are likely to occur in men who are trying hard to demonstrate their masculinity, while unconsciously they would prefer to be passive and dependent.

Hypertension, or high blood pressure, tends to occur in people who have an extremely high amount of hostility, which they go to great lengths to deny and control. It is in such cases that the rising internal pressure from mounting aggression becomes most apparent. These are the hard-driving people who, like Bob Lyons, relentlessly push themselves. They must fight harder and harder to keep aggression in check. The constant containment of aggression requires keeping the defenses at an unusually high level, and therefore we have the phrase "hypertension." Migraine headaches are one indication of hypertension. People who suffer from them tend to be tense, irritable, angry people.

The accident-prone person is often seen as the hapless, helpless victim of circumstances. "Everything happens to him," it seems. He appears as the passive, seemingly non-provoking receiver of pain and anguish. A more careful look shows that the repeated accidents are not quite accidental. He manages to get hurt, redirecting his impulses against himself.

Bodily symptoms, like others, can take extreme forms. Some people spend endless hours and dollars repeatedly seeking various forms of treatment, but avoiding the very treatment that would offer them the best chance of resolving their problems. They are hypochondriacs, and the mode of adaptation, redirection of impulses, is egocentric. They seek multiple operations, demanding that surgeons cut more and more out of them until there is little left to cut. The surgery may be successful, but it cures nothing. The hypochondriac's constant concern with his symptoms provides him with attention, gratifies his dependency needs, and permits him to manipulate his friends and relatives, using his symptoms as an excuse. Though hypochondriacs may manage to go along for many years, they do so at tremendous cost to themselves, particularly in the inhibition of their potential activities and in their inability to enjoy life because so much energy is invested in their symptoms. The following is a case in point:

A middle-aged man has been with his company fifteen years. Over the years he did his work adequately so that his superiors were not very much concerned when he began to develop health problems and take time off. Even now his work is well in hand, so they tolerate his problem, which takes this form. He supervises a large clerical department. He is easily excitable and obviously lives under a strain (ego struggling with containment, overready to respond). He has a history of several stomach operations. He is absent from his job an average of a day a week. He is very much concerned about his own health and that of his family. Both are frequently the subject of his conversation. His associates feel that he is given the status, recognition, and consideration due his position. He has been told his work performance is well regarded by his superiors. He demands considerable recognition (love and attention from others), and feels that he does not get enough of it (always *hungry* for love). As his superiors see it, apparently he wants to be placed in a position where he will get sole credit for some particular activity.

Though close associates regard him highly, many of his subordinates dislike him. He sets high standards for both himself and his subordinates (superego). He spends much of his time communicating with his staff, but most of his communications are self-justifications (appeasing the superego). He knows the language of human relations, but cannot give his subordinates a feeling of warmth (avoidance of feelings). He can pass his own employees in the hall without a word of recognition, apparently lost in his own preoccupations. He tends to display his knowledge to his superiors and to extend himself to fields not his own (self-centered). His higher management avoids him because he demands too much of their time (dependent) and will not confine himself to immediate problems (avoidance).

This dependent, self-centered man would prefer to lean on others stronger than he, but that is neither acceptable nor permissible. He feels inadequately loved, so he must love himself and he has little love to give to others. But how can a man gratify his dependent needs and be cared for in our society? By being sick. It is acceptable to have someone else take care of you when you are sick and to be concerned about your health. His doctors will love him if no one else will.

Obviously, when bodily symptoms become major modes of adaptation and styles of life are built around them, you will not be able to change them. No amount of environmental change will make much difference. If such problems are dealt with at all, they will require professional help. You can prevent their worsening by not placing supervisory demands on people who cannot tolerate having others lean on them, and by having plenty of work for the hard-driving man to do.

CHAPTER 10

Immaturity Reactions

IMMATURITY REACTIONS ARE THOSE FORMS OF BEHAVIOR THAT reflect poor impulse control by the ego. Such behavior results from the ego's inability to delay impulses until they can be appropriately channeled to constructive goals, or from the persistence of childlike attitudes. In either case, the person puts himself and his pleasure first. Immaturity reactions take many forms. Here six types will be considered: those whose major symptoms are impulsiveness, self-centeredness, exploitation of others, passive aggression, inadequacy, and alcoholism. Although all these can be part of other reactions previously described, here we shall review cases in which these symptoms are, to the observer, the most troublesome feature of the personality.

Each of these reactions, except alcoholism, is already an established part of the personality. (Alcoholism can be a symptom of many different conflicts and frequently is a temporary reaction pattern.) Here the subject is personality types rather than acute or chronic reaction patterns.

Rarely do these reactions trouble the victims to the extent of seeking help for their problems. They tend to discharge their anxiety in action. They therefore are not pained enough by their behavior to make consistent efforts to control it by themselves or to seek professional help in dealing with it. This means that, professionally, such people require ego supports in the form of firm controls. Moreover, such people will repeatedly test the controls. Because they are not sufficiently disturbed by their own behavior, no significant changes in behavior are to be expected of them without treatment. In fact, it would be a major effort to motivate them for treatment.

IMPULSIVENESS

In Chapter 3 thought was described as being a "dry run" for action and as a means of delaying an impulse until the ego could find modes of behavior to sublimate the impulse or discharge it in ways that would meet the requirements of the superego and reality. Of course everyone acts impulsively at one time or another. Sometimes external stimulation gives added impetus to the impulse, as when a driver in heavy traffic reacts more angrily than usual to the ineptitude of another driver. The press of internal stimulation may mount when external constrictions are removed, leading to impulsive behavior. Sailors just back from a long voyage tend to "let go" on liberty. People may act impulsively when the possibility of gratification seems too long delayed. Many couples marry hastily in wartime when the man is about to go into service. They also tend to act impulsively when they are so close to obtaining gratification that the tension overcomes the will to wait longer. People returning home after a long trip find the last few miles the hardest to endure, and increase their efforts to get home quickly.

Some people seem to act impulsively much of the time.

For them, it is not an occasional event but a repetitive one. Try as they will, they cannot seem to hold themselves in. The specific impulsive act may vary. Some will talk too much and too long. Some will spend too much of their money on attractive trinkets, which they say they cannot resist. And some will react in rage to the slightest rebuff. When such behavior occurs, it is as if the impulse were so strong that the ego does not have the capacity to modulate it or some parts of the ego are so weak that specific impulses can readily burst through. One such ego weakness is the inability to judge the impact one makes on others, to anticipate the results of what he says or does. The following case is an example:

A thirty-six-year-old man, ten years in his company, has important responsibilities in a service function. He is intelligent, loyal, ambitious, and dependable. He has taken many special courses to improve himself. According to his section chief, he has had difficulty overcoming a certain immaturity and impulsiveness. He is inclined to argue too long after making a point. He conveys the impression of immaturity to other executives. He does not have the poise of his years, and he tends to be over-assertive as well as radical in his opinions, which often turn out to be wrong.

When his chief has talked with him about these problems, he defends himself by saying he is not stubborn but an independent thinker. He excuses his impulsiveness on the basis that everyone is entitled to make mistakes. His criticism of some executives is so open that his chief will not allow him to be in touch with them.

Despite these problems, which have not been solved, he aspires to higher responsibilities. He cannot accept the fact that he has destroyed his opportunities to advance in this organization and that these same difficulties will bar his advancement in another company of the same type.

A man with these characteristics should either be in a company that can tolerate them or have an unusually good boss. With such men who are loyal and conscientious, there is a tendency to assume that they also have adequate ego controls. The corollary assumption is that if they do not act in mature ways, the behavior is temporary and they can correct it if it is pointed out to them. Their supervisors are reluctant to recognize them as immature and to exercise close controls over them. When the man's controls are inadequate, and when the superior does not reinforce the ego with external controls, the impulses simply burst through without adequate refinement.

In such instances the superior can be more helpful by telling the man that the impulsive behavior cannot be permitted on the job. This does not mean that he cannot express himself. Before doing so in public, however, he should talk over his ideas with his superior and think about how he can present them most effectively. Thus his ideas would stand a better chance of being heard and accepted.

If thinking serves to delay impulses and to provide an opportunity for rehearsing actions before they are taken, and if impulsiveness means that that process is short-circuited, then the behavior of the superior is an effort to help make the thinking process operate more fully. This would be a difficult task for the superior, who probably has many other things to do. And because the superior cannot help the man rehearse every situation, from time to time he will continue to act impulsively so that the superior will have to be content with partial success. The superior will have to judge whether his potential value to the firm is worth the effort.

SELF-CENTEREDNESS

Reality dictates that a prudent man should act in his own self-interest. Self-respect requires that a person take his place among others in keeping with his abilities and talents. Most people find that their ultimate self-interest and self-respect depend heavily on their concern for the interest of others. A man's self-interest as a father is served best by his affection for his children, and his self-interest as an executive by his regard for his subordinates. It is fundamental that each person needs to give and to receive affection. It is difficult to receive affection without giving it. When, therefore, a person is unable to give affection, this inability is an indication of inadequate ego development. The person is in effect emotionally malformed.

There are times when most of us act selfishly. There are also times when we are so physically ill or so worried that we simply do not have the energy to be interested in others. When we behave inconsiderately, however, we usually feel guilty about our behavior, and we try to make amends.

But some people appear to act selfishly most of the time and to be unconcerned about it. Or, if they are concerned, often it is because they think someone else is not giving them due recognition or appreciation. When such people turn up in positions of organizational leadership, the results can be disastrous, as this case illustrates:

Vic Williams, at forty-two years of age, was the assistant general manager of a large variety store. He was highly conscious of his good looks and spent much time on his grooming. He had a carefully tended mustache and was always almost too well dressed. After three successful years in his job, he was made manager of another store in the chain.

After a year in his new job, there began to be a flow of complaints to higher management from employees and customers alike about his attitude toward people. At the same time, sales in his store were declining. His record did not compare favorably with the other stores in the chain. Both matters were reviewed with him from time to time.

Williams and his wife were very proud of his position as manager. They seemed to be more interested in establishing their position among the leading citizens of the community than in doing a good job in the store. He devoted so much time to boosting his own stock that it was difficult for employees to see him about operational matters. On many occasions Williams would tell his boss about well-known people in the community with whom he had dined, or played golf, entertained, and how solidly he was entrenched in the best local circles. When the boss later talked with some of the community leaders about Williams' contribution to the business community as a store manager, several of these men did not recall having met him and some did not even know his name.

Since the morale of the employees was at a low ebb, and volume and profits were declining, Mr. Williams was asked to resign.

As was indicated in Chapter 4, one way to deal with the constructive drive is to turn it back on oneself. This results in self-centeredness and self-inflation. It also means that the person has less energy to invest in other people, for he is putting so much in himself. If a person is unable to give his affection to others in useful ways, but must keep it for himself, and if he seeks to make others admire him, we can infer that for some reason unknown to us he must feel unloved.

In this case, it is interesting to note that apparently Mr. Williams' self-centeredness was unnoticed by his superiors. Then, when his ordinary behavior became exaggerated under the pressure of his new job, it must have been in a desperate effort to cover over his deep feelings of inadequacy in this situation and, furthermore, to get himself out of the situation. Since self-centered behavior is highly unlikely to begin at age forty-two—and such behavior was evident in the way he was overconcerned about his appearance—his superiors obviously did not try to understand the meaning of his behavior before they promoted him. They therefore share the responsibility for his failure.

The immaturity of self-centered behavior suggests that these people cannot operate well in situations where others depend on them to carry on alone. They are too dependent themselves to do so. They need a superior to lean on, one who will provide them and their subordinates a source of approval, affection, and esteem.

EXPLOITATION OF OTHERS

It is only a short psychological step from being self-centered to exploiting others. But exploitation obviously invites retribution. Eventually those who are exploited will rebel. In the long run, therefore, exploitation is always self-destructive, whether on an international level as in colonialism, on a business level as in practices that led to the development of labor unions, or in individual relationships.

When exploitation is a conspicuous component of self-centeredness, the self-destructive aspects of a person's behavior often seem to overshadow his self-centeredness. The diffusion of his aggression is even more conspicuous. These people do not hold themselves in high esteem, for while they devote considerable effort to seeking approval, they devote more energy to attacking others. Often, it seems, they invite the condemnation and rejection of their colleagues.

It is as if, thinking themselves unworthy, they go about proving that thesis. Yet, in an almost pitiful effort to maintain some feelings of worthiness, they love themselves.

In venting their aggression, they leave considerable emotional distress in their wake and are destructive to the organization as well as to themselves. Again this shows how mental illness is communicated and how the illness of the person can have detrimental effects on the organization, although many organizations put up with this behavior a long time. This case is a good example:

A man in middle management has been with his company twenty years and heads a department of four divisions and two hundred people. He is technically well qualified. He should be a valuable asset, but his colleagues find him extremely difficult to work with. Though he is loyal to the organization and has good intellectual ability, his behavior often hurts the company's reputation.

He has expensive tastes in food and clothing. He is meticulous about his appearance and is a "big tipper." He will not be seen in public places beneath his standards. He is rough on service people in public places. He abuses and criticizes them aggressively. As a result, he has been asked not to return to certain places. Though he is married, he frequently appears in public with a woman who is also married.

He is afraid of embarrassment or criticism about his performance. He often has his staff do hours of work to answer a minor question. He demands of them more than they are paid for. He magnifies details and calls meetings for the sake of meetings. He directs his temper outbursts to his subordinates and harasses them with petty constrictions, but can "turn on the charm." In short, he manipulates people for his own ends without regard for their feelings or respect for them as individuals. If someone resists being exploited in this way, and asks for a transfer, the manager has a temper tantrum.

When these matters are called to his attention, he evades the discussion by diversionary tacts. Because of his tenure and good showing in a few areas, the company has put up with this behavior.

As long as no one confronts this man directly with the fact that he is exploiting and abusing people, or insists that he control his behavior or give up his job, he will continue to be destructive to himself, his subordinates, and his organization. The manager is a long way from meeting the standards of his ego ideal (afraid of embarrassment or criticism of his performance). He relieves his guilt feelings by making others the targets of his poorly controlled aggression. He thus creates an illusion for himself that he is a powerful person, and that, too, helps relieve his feelings of inadequacy. Though apparently self-centered, he is also self-destructive, for he flaunts conventional mores publicly, which, together with his other negative behavior, will eventually cause some reaction from his superiors. In some ways, he acts as if he is daring his superiors to do something about his behavior, which is another way of being self-destructive.

But his callous disregard for and manipulation of others who are weaker than he is a hallmark of his personality. This shows that the drives are inadequately fused and indicates an overreaction to internal stresses. He may need more recognition, esteem, and approval than he is getting, but this is no excuse for permitting him to indulge in this kind of displacement. A responsible position requires a responsible person. If he cannot carry the responsibility for his own behavior, then the organization must do so, or get someone else to do the job.

PASSIVE AGGRESSION

Among enlisted men in the army the most effective device for frustrating officers is to do exactly what they say—nothing more, nothing less. Since officers cannot direct every action, and the enlisted man has obeyed his orders to the letter, the task is inadequately done, but the enlisted man is safe. Children have a variant of the same device: They frequently manage not to hear what their parents have to say. Both behaviors are passive. The enlisted men do no more than they are told to do, and the children do nothing at all. Both behaviors are aggressive because they are intended to flout authority. And both occur among adults in business organizations, typified by this example:

A plant manager, an engineer of twenty-two-years' service in a wide range of positions is a likable chap. He is strongly inclined to maintain the status quo. The vice-president in charge of manufacturing has asked him to delineate the goals he wants to reach both in the near and more distant future. He responded very generally with goals that were easy to obtain or were nonquantitative. Some of his goals should have included specific improvements in the plant. He is not only slow to agree about the need for improvements, but even slower to make recommendations. Reluctantly he agreed to draw up plans for making physical improvements. Two deadlines have passed without the plans.

The vice-president feels that the plant manager is far more capable than he appears. When pressured, he promises to do a job, but then does not follow through on time. He more often misses a deadline than meets one. He conveys the feeling to the vice-president that he is playing a game; if only he humors the vice-president, maybe the vice-president will go away.

Failure to act when necessary under these conditions is a form of aggression, no matter how much the person tries to cover it over. It becomes particularly irritating when the man is generally quite capable. This problem can be either a style of behavior, in which case the behavior has been recurrent, or it may be in response to a previous authoritarian management. If, as in this case, it has been going on a long time, little change will be brought about by the vice-president. If the engineer has learned not to demonstrate initiative as a result of authoritarian management, then there is the possibility that the vice-president can help him direct his aggression into the task instead of into passive resistance.

To differentiate between these two problems, the vice-president would do well to talk with his plant manager and to find out how he feels about his position. If he has been subject to authoritarian leadership, the vice-president will have to take considerable time to assure him that he will not be jeopardizing his position by assuming initiative and even by making mistakes. In this discussion, the vice-president will have to make clear what his own responsibilities are and his requirements of the plant manager. That is, he will have to make the realities of the situation clear so that the ego can act on the basis of reality, to whatever extent that is possible. At the same time, he will have to demonstrate to the plant manager that he is an ally in getting the job done, for which both have a responsibility. With increasing trust, the manager may be able to lead. Without it, he can only resist to protect himself.

Parenthetically, passive aggression is a commonplace defense of middle management. It is a form of denial or avoidance. This is particularly likely to be a favored middle-management technique for both cultural and practical reasons. Culturally, passive aggressors tend to be middle class. With their strongly developed superegos, middle-class people frequently feel that open expressions of aggression are not appropriate. Rather than express their dissatisfaction directly, they do so passively.

Some people have a gift for making others angry at them, but by appearing to be so helplessly inadequate, they cause those who are angry to feel guilty. They are so ingenuous about their provocation, and so often accompany it with a smile, that higher management who raise questions about their performance may well end by feeling that the failure of the middle-management man to perform is their fault. This man is an example:

A young staff man has the job of preparing studies that outline alternative courses of action which his superiors are considering. He also must present his findings in meetings. He has a good command of words and his reports show solid data. When he presents his reports, he pontificates and often wanders in verbal circles. His reports are notable for unnecessary detail. His manner is often that of a high school senior delivering a valedictory address. His pontification, circumlocution, and unmanliness anger the superiors to whom he is reporting. From time to time they have told him they want information brief and to the point and without pontification. He promises repeatedly that he will do better, and to a limited degree, he has. Some want to fire him, but others point out that he is such a nice fellow, he tries so hard, and he is so obviously sincere that they want to keep him. Besides, they say, who else would employ him? Those who want to keep him have stopped trying to improve him, but they still get angry and demonstrate their anger by the contemptuous, disdainful manner in which they treat him. He might just as well be a high school senior for all of the respect they have for him.

Practically speaking, the middle-management man often plays it safe by not acting. If, as in some plants, top management moves every year or so, the middle-management man does just as well to maintain the status quo. The people who demand changes will go after a while and he will still be responsible for his end of the job.

Passive aggression should be examined to see whether it is a temporary or long-term phenomenon. The next question is whether it is related to a culturally determined mode of handling aggression or more simply to the realities of the situation. In any event, the matter can be dealt with only if it is recognized.

INADEQUACY

Some people seem to be just unable to "make it." They are not retarded or necessarily unintelligent. Rather, it seems as if they have never developed the ability to cope with the everyday responsibilities that everyone has. They seem to live a marginal existence, always on the edge of things and never very effective about anything. Their inadequacy is conspicuous, so they are rarely promoted, for the next job is too big for them. For them, sheer survival seems to be a major accomplishment. With support from their supervisors and their families, they are sometimes able to meet simple and specific demands. Left to their own devices, they evade and avoid, or by means of compensation, try to hide their inadequacy by being aggressive to others. Here is a case in point:

A man was employed by a field office of a large petroleum company in a minor clerical position. Shortly after employment he was moved to a slightly higher position in which he had the responsibility for maintaining simple statistical tables. This job brought him into contact with the top executives of the company for whom the data were gathered. Almost from the beginning of his contact with them, he developed a "big shot" complex. Soon he was insisting that he not be called by his first name and instead be addressed as "Mr." This became almost an obsession with him. As he grew older, if younger employees did not treat him in ways he regarded as respectful, he would reprimand them. Most people learned to avoid him.

He developed a knack for appearing busy all the time. He could stretch the most trivial task to a full day's work. He came to work an hour early in the morning and left an hour early in the afternoon. He felt that his was a privileged position and that he could adjust his hours to suit himself. He was given the responsibility for supervising the larger operation of which he was a part, but he was soon relieved of that position because he could not get along with people. He was relegated to an even more obscure data-compiling job. He continued to express the feeling that he was better qualified than others who had advanced. When there was a retrenchment, he was the first to be fired and is now on relief.

Such a person needs step-by-step direction. The ego is not adequate to cope with complexity, and usually it carries a heavy load of guilt feelings. If you imagine a person like this in the process of growing up, and think of all the chiding and exploitation he must experience, it is easy to see that he can feel inadequate just because he *is* so inadequate. He is likely to know his shortcomings only too well. If step-by-step direction can be accompanied by ordinary give and take between him and his supervisors, which makes him feel an accepted part of things, then his superego pressures will tend to diminish. Such a person can be told directly and in a kindly manner if his behavior is inappropriate, and he will usually strive to please. This places a heavy burden on a supervisor. The question of whether the results are worth the effort is something the boss will have to decide for himself. If, however, such a person is not adequately supervised, as he was not in this case, he will get into difficulties and fail.

ALCOHOLISM

Though alcoholism is regarded by many physicians and laymen as a disease, and many recovered alcoholics would like to think of it as such, it is not a disease. It is a symptom that occurs in conjunction with many different kinds of disequilibrium.

Some authorities believe there is a physiological suscepti-
bility that contributes to alcoholism, but these aspects of
the problem are vague and poorly understood. For all practical treatment purposes, alcoholism is a psychological symptom, and the most effective means of dealing with it are
psychological.

A man may try to escape environmental problems by getting drunk, and social drinking is used by many as a way to
ease the day's tensions. He may also be trying to avoid the
pain of depression or the severe anxiety of an ego whose
controls are tenuous. Whatever problem the alcoholic is
trying to deal with, his mode of coping with it is regressive.
That is, symptomatically he is returning to the bottle. One
consequence of drinking is to become helpless (for others
must take care of the alcoholic when he is drunk) and to
withdraw from the outside world. Another is to become
more primitively aggressive. In short, the ego is soluble in
alcohol. Neither of these behaviors is oriented to reality, for
to become drunk is to evade and avoid problems rather
than come to grips with them. Unchecked alcoholism is slow
suicide.

Between 2 and 3 per cent of all men between thirty-five
and fifty-five have a drinking problem, according to best
estimates, though accurate statistics are hard to come by.
Until the relatively recent advent of Alcoholics Anonymous
and such drugs as antabuse, the only treatment available to
most alcoholics was "drying out," or rest cure.

Because alcoholism may mask many more difficult problems, it is not enough in many cases merely to dry out the
alcoholic. Other symptoms may take the place of the drinking. Furthermore, rehabilitation of the man with a severe
drinking symptom usually requires help for his wife as well,
for clinical experience shows that his relationship with her

is an important component of his problem. Some wives prefer the martyrdom of having an alcoholic husband. The wife and children who must cope with such a person over a long period of time usually have a difficult and painful emotional experience and as a result, they too need help. There are now adjuncts of AA to provide support for wives and children of alcoholics. In this sense, too, mental illness is a communicable disease.

Only within the preceding decade has industry taken an active part in dealing with this problem. Up to that time, most business executives denied they had problems with those who drank too much. However, leaders in business and industry have now come to recognize that they pay a price for the alcoholic, but even more important, that they can help in motivating an alcoholic to seek help. In fact, in addition to his personal problem, another problem of the alcoholic in industry is the procrastination of his superiors in facing up to the problem he creates. It is not unusual for reluctant executives to allow such problems to go on for years. Procrastination merely fosters the self-destruction of the alcoholic.

There are many good company programs for dealing with alcoholism. The best is that conducted at University Hospital in New York under the auspices of Consolidated Edison and nearly a score of other companies, through which comprehensive medical and psychiatric services are available. Unfortunately, this program seems to be limited in its participation to hourly employees. Other company programs may be conducted in conjunction with local alcoholism clinics and Alcoholics Anonymous. All depend on a formally structure procedure for dealing with the problem. The more successful programs claim a recovery rate as high as 70 per cent.[7]

These programs require a simple formula which communicates to the alcoholic that the company and his superiors care about him but that they cannot permit him to be destructive to himself or the company. When such a problem arises, the alcoholic should be told that despite his likely denials, he has a problem. He should be told further that he must deal with the problem, either through established channels or on his own. If he does not seek professional help and becomes intoxicated again, he will lose his job. If he does seek professional help, and if his drinking continues to interfere with his job, he will be placed on sick leave according to whatever provisions the company has for any severe or chronic illness. When his physician says that he has recovered from his symptoms and is able to work again, then he will be permitted to return to his job.

When the company moves to support the ego of the alcoholic by confronting him with reality and limiting his alternatives, this often moves him to seek help. However, the company must take its firm position early in the course of the developing symptom or its leverage as a force to motivate the man will be lost. When a man has become so addicted to alcohol that his job means little to him, company policy loses its usefulness.

The policy enunciated here is similar to that for any serious illness that threatened the man or the organization. In most companies, such illnesses as tuberculosis or heart disease would be handled the same way. Thus the policy enunciated is neither harsh nor unkind, but simply uses reality as a basis for judgment and action.

Help in the development of company programs for dealing with alcoholism is available from the National Council on Alcoholism, 2 East 103rd Street, New York 29, New York, and its 75 local committees across the country. Additional help is available from state commissions or agencies on alcoholism. An excellent comprehensive guide to programs and policies for dealing with alcoholism has recently been prepared for the Smithers Foundation by Professor Harrison M. Trice of Cornell.[8] Every executive and occupational physician should have a copy.

PART III

PROBLEMS IN CONTEXT

JUST AS THERE ARE A NUMBER OF TYPICAL REACTION PATTERNS TO stress, which were discussed in Part II, so there are also a number of typical psychological *arenas* for adults in our culture, dynamically related to the discussion in Part I. These are dimensions of life in which psychological struggle or conflict are common experience. Here, we shall focus our four arenas of adult life as they occur in the course of a man's relationship with his work organization: identity problems, advancement problems, family problems, and age problems.

Each one of these is intertwined with work and complicated by the demands, requirements, and values of the work organization, particularly for men in managerial ranks. These problems are far less pressing for women in connection with work, in part because there are relatively few women in managerial ranks and in part because women have well-defined roles as wives and mothers, which usually take precedence over their work roles.

Our concern with these problems is to recognize them, to anticipate them, to soften some of their impact, and to mobilize the resources of the organization to help the person who is under stress. Though everyone must face these problems, most people can cope with them reasonably well. When an executive is aware of them and acts accordingly to help someone, he saves both himself and his organization considerable later turmoil, disappointment, and heartache. In short, this part will discuss the prevention of distress—for both the person and the organization.

CHAPTER 11

Identity Problems

Psychologically speaking, a person matures when the
ego is in effective control of the personality and manages to
synthesize the ego, id, and superego forces into a relatively
harmonious whole. However, psychological maturity does
not mean the end of psychological growth, for when and if
the ego is master, then the person enjoys living, makes good
use of his capacities and talents, is comfortable with himself and others, and is able to cope with stress. He knows
who he is and what he wants to do with himself.

Identification is a major mechanism in growth, as was
indicated in Chapter 3. In the process of growing up, a boy
or girl identifies himself to varying degrees with many different people—the parents, grandparents, teachers, friends,
older brothers and sisters, ministers, and so on. Some are
real people; some, childhood storied heroes. Each is different
from the others in some ways. The values of one may be
incompatible with those of another.

Before he reaches psychological maturity, the youngster
must organize and consolidate these many identifications.
He may reject some, accept others in part, and recognize

others only slightly. He does so in the light of his own needs and experiences. As a result, out of these many identifications, he produces something new and something more than all of them added together: a unique, well-integrated self.[9]

When that psychological task has been accomplished, the person has found effective ways of channeling his drives in constructive activity, in keeping with his abilities and the realities of his environment. A man's occupation therefore is one major way through which the ego can solidify itself, and if his occupation serves that purpose, success in work reflects the integration of the many forces of the personality.

A man's struggle to establish his identity is the critical struggle of young adulthood. For many young people it is not easily resolved. It is a commonplace among college students that they are very much concerned with what they should be and what they should do. Nor is it unusual to find many young men and women who have completed college and who have even embarked on careers and are still struggling with their doubts and indecisions about who and what they are. Some never do find out.

Identity conflict seems to be a more acute struggle in our culture than it was a hundred years ago or is in some other countries where social class lines are more stratified. Here, the relatively free movement from one social class to another and among various occupations offers a young person many choices of identification figures and occupations. Where there is choice, there must be decision. And when a person must decide for *himself* who *he* is, he has only himself to fall back on. It is easy for a man to know his identity, his place in society, and what his life work will be if he is required by custom to limit his horizons or to pursue the same work as his father. It is much harder when he has to assess himself and fit himself into a constantly changing social scene. Here is a case in point:

Leon Rupp, now thirty-two years old, is one of four sons of a highly successful hardware wholesaler. From very early in life his two older brothers took an interest in the father's business. When they went to college, they took business administration with the avowed intention of taking over the business. With Leon it was different. He was his mother's favorite and through him she sought to fulfill her own musical aspirations, which had been cut short by her marriage. Leon was highly talented and an apt pupil. His violin virtuosity was recognized while he was yet in high school. He won a scholarship to a major university, but after two years, he dropped out. He did not quite know why he dropped out. It just did not seem to be what he wanted to do, he said. His disappointed mother urged him to return home. His father, as if relieved that the musical nonsense was over, urged him to take his place in the business. Leon refused. Instead, he stayed in Chicago, where he took one mediocre job after another. None had a future for him, for almost all were marginal selling jobs. After a year and a half of being on his own unsuccessfully, Leon gave in to his parents' urgings and returned home to the business. He feigned his old sense of humor, but it was apparent that his sparkle was gone. He did not even touch his violin. He married, was divorced, and married again in a two-year period. He goes to business every day, but he longs to leave it. Chances are he never will.

This example highlights some of the sources of conflicts and the symptomatic results. Leon is still wondering whether to do what he wants or what his parents want, whether to be the prodigy his mother wants or the businessman his father wants. He could not satisfy both his mother and father, so after considerable doubt, he chose to identify with his father. He is not using his talents as he might, either for music or business. He is not the unique Leon he set out to be—Leon the violin virtuoso. He is now Leon the businessman—the man he never wanted to be.

When identity is not successfully consolidated, the resulting stress leads to inadequate work performance. In contrast to other stress situations where work performance is impaired, in this case it does not reach levels that the person's capacity seemed to promise. Usually, the young person cannot concentrate consistently on what he is doing or, to fight off distracting thoughts, he may devote much of his attention to a small and relatively insignificant part of his job, or move too quickly from one interest to another without really developing any. It is as if, unable to deal with the larger problem, he tackles a tiny one with ferocious intensity or spreads his energy among many. He shies away from competition, as if to show that he does not feel up to taking it on. Cynically, he rejects what to others appear to be good opportunities. For him, they are to be scorned. Inside himself he feels inadequate and immature, for he is such a long way from his ego ideal. Despite his youth, he feels often that he has not used his potential capabilities and that he will not ever be really able to do so.

He is often not sure what he wants to do. He limits his interest in many things, since without a clear conception of himself, it is difficult to relate new experiences to a core of personality. He may therefore take up many interests and drop them quickly. When he is required to study or work, often he will have to force himself to be involved in what he is doing; as a result, his performance will be inadequate, though he has the potential ability for doing more and better work.

These activities will, of course, leave him frustrated because there is so little satisfaction in any of them. He will therefore tend to be angry with himself and with others. Without a clear conception of where he is going, in the sense that he has certain skills and talents that he will continue to make use of, he is likely to be afraid of the future and of responsibility. As a result, he will tend to withdraw from others, either by hostility toward them or by pulling further into himself.

With these feelings, it is difficult for him to establish warm and continuous relationships with other people. He avoids others because, not quite knowing who he is, he does not know how he should act toward others. He has difficulty leading and equal difficulty following. Sometimes he chooses companions far beneath him in intelligence, ability, and social sophistication because he does not feel capable of meeting his own and others' expectations. The experienced executive will see in this description many a young man with precocious promise who simply petered out after he was hired.

The reasons identity is not crystallized are numerous. We have touched on conflicting identifications and wishes, and the looseness of supporting social structure. Invariably there are other unconscious conflicts and external social pressures that make self-integration difficult.

The identity struggle is made more acute in our culture by the constant pressure on young people to decide early what they are going to be. This pressure begins when the small child is asked repeatedly what he is going to be when he grows up. It is not resolved here as in some European countries where academic authorities decide when the child finishes elementary school whether he will be eligible for trade school or the university. Instead, everyone is expected to go through high school (witness our concern with drop-outs). In high school there is an increasing emphasis on vocational guidance, with constant pressure on adolescents to make occupational choices. Few fully understand the actual work of their fathers, so identification with the father's work is difficult. Most have had little experience on which to base choices. But nevertheless they feel pressed to choose.

Underlying this pressure is the tacit social fiction that for every person there is a specific occupational role which fits his abilities and needs, as if a man were born foreordained to fit a socially defined niche. This is often expressed in the idea that the purpose of vocational guidance is to fit square pegs into square holes.

As a matter of fact, most people can do a number of things well. It was a standing joke in the army during World War II that no man was ever assigned to something he knew. The range of possibilities is so great that it is not easy to choose among them, particularly when one has had limited experience. This makes it harder to attain identity. Yet occupation is a necessary part of identity.

As a result, when young men (and to a lesser extent young women) come into business organizations (or church, education, or government organizations as well), they are often still struggling with the problem of identity. Among ministers the critical point in this struggle seems to come about the third year of pastoral work.

But in our culture, it is not considered acceptable for an adult to admit to his colleagues and bosses that he is unsure about his career choices. Realistically, in many organizations it may be unwise for him to do so because his superiors may then favor his rivals or later use his doubts as a weapon against him. Furthermore, having been under pressure for many years to make a firm occupational decision, he often feels guilty for not having done so. Thus the identity strug-

gle, compounded by feelings of guilt and the inherent rivalry
of the business situation, is widespread among young people
relatively new to their work organizations. But it is rarely
recognized and dealt with openly by their superiors.

Many young people are able to resolve this problem by
themselves. The case of a young physicist turned plant
manager is illustrative:

> He had had an interest in science from high school
> days. In college he soon became the favorite of the
> physics professor. That in itself was an achievement for
> him, for his father was a railroad brakeman. With the
> endorsement of his professor, he was awarded a fellow-
> ship in physics in a large university, and after getting
> his Ph.D., he entered the research laboratory of a fa-
> mous company. For a few years he was intrigued with
> what he was doing, but he soon realized that he would
> not make any major contributions as a physicist. True,
> he was a good enough journeyman physicist, but he did
> not have the spark of creativity that would make him
> a great one. As he struggled with this problem, he de-
> cided that as long as he was going to be only a plodding
> physicist, he would do better to turn to a managerial
> career where his knowledge of physics would make him
> a highly demanded and well-paid executive. This, how-
> ever, involved a painful reappraisal of himself. Fortu-
> nately, his own organization was always looking for new
> managerial talent and had channels through which he
> could evaluate his managerial potential and effect a
> change. Though he did well as a manager, a year after
> the change he was still occasionally expressing his re-
> gret that he was not able to fulfill his early promise as a
> physicist.

Although many can resolve this problem by themselves, for others the problem is conspicuous in the form of erratic behavior and the feeling that, "I just can't find myself." It is easy to see such young people as malcontents, rather than as going through a period of evolution. You may be simultaneously angry with and disappointed in them, particularly if they do not seem to correct their behavior after a problem has been pointed out to them. But you usually have enough invested in a young man to make it worth your while to pay some attention to what is going on, and you might even be able to assure that such problems come to your attention early.

If you have to do with recruiting, placing, or supervising young men new to the organization, you might communicate in early interviews that you are aware that most young people are still in the process of making their major career decisions. If they decide to stay with your organization, of course you will be pleased. If, however, they make another choice which is better for them, then in the long run that will be better for the organization, too. In your own self-interest, you should be available to talk with them about this problem, as you would be about any other job problem.

It is important for you to communicate to those who do seek help that the problem is commonplace, that many people in their twenties and some who are older have the same problem. There is no reason for shame or embarrassment about a conflict that everyone has to resolve sooner or later. The opportunity to get the problem out in the open, without any risk that to admit a problem will later backfire, and to look at it with an experienced older person will make it easier to resolve.

In talking with a young man about this problem, it will be useful to keep four realities in mind:

1. Currently there is a strong pressure among young people and from their parents to attain identity by age twenty or so, and to feel that once one has made a decision, that is *it*. The culture tends to push people into niches of its structure to make sure they settle down. But genuine identity is achieved by evolution. It does not result from high-pressure molding techniques. Among the most creative people, it is likely to continue evolving. When a group of scientists introduced themselves publicly to each other at a recent meeting, several said, "I don't know what I am." By this they meant they had started out as physicists or biologists, but by following their interests, they had come upon new problems that did not fit neatly into already defined fields. Certainly they identified themselves as scientists, but that identity left much room for further evolution.

2. People are a combination of capacities, talents, and skills, all of which work together. Any organization that employs a man has a use for some of what he has to offer. Few organizations can make *full* use of his skills and potentials. As a result, many people feel that they are wasting much of themselves, and many executives devoutly (and futilely) wish that people would be content to do just that one thing they are doing well. That cannot be.

3. The organization needs people who can change with changing circumstances and opportunities. It requires flexible people who have not decided at twenty *exactly* what they are going to do for the rest of their lives. It must therefore not encourage rigidity or overidentification with a specific task or unit. This means that the company will have to be patient with the indecisiveness of promising people as they evolve their respective identities.

4. When the organization does not force people into molds, but instead encourages the development and use of poten-

tial, some people will develop skills they never knew they had. This is true even of people in middle age. It is impressive, for example, how many middle-aged women who go to work for the first time seem to blossom out as they discover new facets of themselves. And it is an old story that people never know to what heights they can rise until they are given a challenge.

Keep these considerations in mind as you hear the young person out so that he can realize that you understand his problem. If he can feel he trusts you, this will be an important support in his efforts to resolve his problem. Such support will relieve some of his anxiety and guilt, and make it less necessary for him to devote so much of his energy to maintaining a protective façade. He will not have to continue making believe he has no problem in order to appear adult to you.

An established identity is the smoothest way each of us has of handling the pressures of the id, the demands of the superego, and the contingencies of the environment. The more a man is certain of his identity, the more he defines it by activity as a friend, a husband, a competitor, a manager.

Two other conflicts take place in relation to work, which are complementary struggles to the identity conflict when a person enters the employ of an organization. The first of these is the issue of identification with the organization and the second has to do with values.

IDENTIFICATION WITH THE ORGANIZATION

Very early in his managerial career, a young man must decide whether he is going to stay in that organization or go to another. This choice problem is compounded by two pressures.

One is the widespread practice in business and industry, particularly in larger, more stable businesses, toward promotion from within. This discourages movement from one organization to another except for those at the highest and lowest levels and for highly specialized personnel. After a limited period of training as a management trainee, a man is expected to move on in management ranks. He cannot, after a few years, easily move to another company and begin again as a management trainee, for he is then too old to start anew.

The second pressure is the need to have a consistent work record. A man who moves several times to different companies is soon likely to be looked upon as a job hopper. Unless with each move he also acquires more skills and greater responsibilities, he will move from job to job at the same relative level, usually in small organizations, thus losing opportunities to move upward in the managerial hierarchy.

In a phrase, the young man newly started on his management career must decide quickly whether he will put all his occupational eggs in one corporate basket. If he does so, he will probably have to stick with his decision thereafter, for if he later decides to change, chances are that he will have to go to a smaller organization which does not operate on the principle of promotion from within, or to start a business of his own.

This struggle, too, usually goes unrecognized by superiors in the organization. While some are aware that there is such a problem, most try to convince the young man that his future lies in the organization. They would act more wisely in the interests of both the company and the man if, again, they created an atmosphere of trust and confidence within which they could help him examine his problem. Under such circumstances, his decision would probably be more sound. If he decided to go, then probably both he and the company would be much better off than if he stayed half-heartedly.

This problem, too, should be recognized as a universal one in organizations. The young man should be helped to recognize that he need not feel guilty because he has doubts about staying. There is nothing wrong with asking himself about his future directions. It is not disloyal to feel that he might have better opportunities elsewhere.

A successful consultant, now middle aged, tells this story on himself. As a young paint salesman, he was asked by the sales vice-president of his company about his future plans. Flushed with his initial sales successes and enthusiastic about his company, he told the vice-president he intended to stay in that company and work his way to the top. He was startled to see that he had not made the right impression on the vice-president. The older man shook his head. "You don't have to please me," he said, "and you might even make a mistake. I was in three other companies before I found the right one." Sobered by this comment, the young salesman had second thoughts. He then made the most important occupational decision of his life. He went back to school for professional training. His present position as a respected consultant brings him far more gratification than he could have had in his old company, and, indeed, he makes a greater contribution to the business community as a whole. Probably, he says, he would not have moved if the older, wiser man had not encouraged him to lay his psychological cards on the table and had not given him a realistic basis for decision.

VALUE CONFLICTS

Another facet of the struggle for identity is the problem of conflicting values. At an unconscious level, this problem is part of the process of selecting and reorganizing identifications into a unified whole. In doing so, a person introjects some values to varying degrees, and rejects others. At a conscious level, however, it is a reality problem, and it is this aspect that is relevant to the organization. Of course conflicting values are characteristic of our whole culture; so, such conflicts are not limited to companies or churches or governmental agencies. The culture is simultaneously idealistic and materialistic, generous and selfish, supportive and destructive. Brotherly love is preached from the pulpit; "Don't be a softie or a sucker," is the underlying byword in business. Cooperation is taught in the classroom and athletic competition is intended to teach good sportsmanship. Cooperation in the business world, however, is often a matter of the more powerful person in the organizational hierarchy demanding compliance, and competition means "destroy the opposition if you can"—whether the opposition is someone whose job you want or a company whose markets you want. The concept of fairness often gives way to *caveat emptor* and the devil take the hindmost.

Value conflicts tend to fall within at least four major dimensions in business and industry, with considerable overlap among the dimensions. The degree of conflict varies significantly from person to person.

1. *Human-nonhuman Orientation.* In many organizations it is quite obvious that far more consideration is given to things—machines, statistics, advertising—than to people. In most organizations, once the minimal conditions of personnel policies and reasonably adequate working facilities have

been met, people tend to be taken for granted. Though there is considerable emphasis on the teaching of human relations in supervisory and management courses, rarely is this emphasis put into practice. Thus young men in management, particularly, tend to be caught up in the conflict between human and nonhuman values. It is not unusual for an executive to say facetiously, "Everything would be fine if we didn't have people." Such a remark clearly shows where that executive's focus is and what demands he will make on his subordinates. If, in addition, the organization exploits people, then the conflict for some young men will become an acute one. This quotation highlights a continuing conflict about these two values in a major American business:

"It's [business games] really a way to adjust your mind to top management," explains one [company] executive. "The quicker you start to think of a business problem as a thing without human beings, the better you'll do." *

2. *Self-others Orientation.* There is a continuous argument in the management literature about the reason for the existence of business organizations. Some say they exist to make a profit, all the profit they can; others assert the organization has many social functions to perform, and profit is only one of these. The argument becomes directly relevant to everyday business life and to values when there is a continuing flow of Federal Trade Commission complaints about deception and dishonesty in packaging, guarantees, and advertising, and with the concept of planned obsolescence in products.

Reared in a culture that officially advocates fair play, honesty, and integrity, a young management man raises many questions about himself and his organization. A good

* *Time,* Sept. 8, 1961, p. 82.

many wonder how to justify themselves if they are not giving their customers value for money received, or if they are urged to get all they can for themselves, regardless of means. Some quickly aver that, "You have to be crooked to survive in business," but more wonder whether they really do have to be dishonest to succeed. At least one professor flatly takes the former position:

Atlantic City, N. J.—(AP) Honesty and business success are "not always compatible," a University of Notre Dame professor, Dr. Herbert Johnston, told the National Conference of Catholic Men's convention here. "It may be that, in this job or that business, you simply cannot succeed and stay honest," he said.*

Louis Cabot, president of the Cabot Company, lists these common practices which exemplify this dimension of the value conflict: useless products, misleading advertising, secret rebates, false list prices, extravagant gifts to purchasing agents, hiring lawyers to break contracts whose original intent is clear, investing in favorite suppliers, padding expense accounts, and successfully avoiding taxes.[10]

The question of whom to put first, oneself or the customer, the colleague or the government, is then no idle one. Given our kind of culture with heavy superego reinforcement, it can become a pressing one.

3. *Aggression-affection Orientation.* When a young man enters an organization with the anticipation, heavily emphasized by recruiters, that he will be helped to grow into a mature and responsible executive, he expects just that— training, experience, and support in the growth process. He may quickly learn, however, that "opportunity" means opportunity to fight his way up, and, further, that every trick goes and nobody asks questions as long as he gets results.

* Topeka *Capital-Journal,* June 30, 1963.

When 1,700 businessmen were asked if they were ethical, they said they were, but when they were asked if other businessmen were equally ethical, they doubted it. They thought the average businessman would pad expense accounts, take advantage of inside information to make a killing on the stock market, and raid other company's employees to learn top secrets. Most knew of bribery, price fixing, and supplying call girls to customers. In their view, personal ethics give way to the demands of the business because the individual cannot defy the company and still keep his job.[11]

When, instead of getting support and regard, the prospective executive finds himself pressured to be an instrument of aggression, he may well question whether it was wise to have chosen a business organization for his career.

4. *Idealistic-materialistic Orientation.* The rising standard of living in this country has diminished the importance of money as the prime motivator of men. People more frequently ask themselves what they want to do with their working lives and in what ways they can make a contribution to society. They more often have a feeling that they want their effort to have some social meaning as well as be a way to earn a livelihood. This thesis was most apparent when the first group of Peace Corps volunteers returned from their overseas stints. Despite the attempts of business organizations to employ them, almost all chose to pursue public careers. Nor is this concern limited to young people. Many executives who have accumulated wealth as they have achieved their occupational goals ask themselves, "Now what?" Some merely struggle with this question. Others leave business organizations because they cannot fulfill their idealistic goals there, even though they have organizational and leadership abilities. This is a case in point:

An enterprising young man, after considerable screening, was employed as a customer's man in a stock brokerage firm. Despite his zeal and energy, he was not very successful as a salesman of stocks and bonds. Both he and his employers were disappointed with his sales record. He left the firm to enter the ministry. In a few short years with a metropolitan church, he had one of the largest congregations and most magnificent new church edifices in that community. He had the talents for which he had been employed in the brokerage firm, but there was no way in the organization to use these talents in keeping with his values.

The most painful feature of many conscious value conflicts is their chronicity. They continue to rub the wrong way, grinding, irritating, and stimulating hostility. Sometimes this occurs because the facets of the conflict are not sufficiently clear for a decision to be made about it, to take one side or another. Sometimes it occurs because superiors make conflicting demands. Lower-level supervisors characteristically suffer from the second problem. They are told repeatedly that they are responsible for good human relations with line employees. They are given all kinds of courses on human relations. They are also held accountable for pressuring employees into productivity and are often so bound by policies and procedures that they are allowed little flexibility to use their own judgment. As a result, sometimes their guilt is increased and their work performance falls off. They know what they ought to be doing in their relationships with their employees, but the very pressures exerted by management make it impossible for them to do so in most cases.[12] Only their guilt grows.

These examples could be multiplied a thousandfold: government employees who must yield expert judgment to political considerations; insurance salesmen who are promoted to the public as estate counselors, but who must sell high-premium coverage to make their commission goals; advertising men who must make the most banal products attractive to the customer (it should not be surprising that many ad men write books attacking advertising and business in general); engineers are asked to shortcut quality in products so that they will wear out quickly; and so on.

Right and wrong are often easy to define when one is not directly involved in a situation. In most cases, however, the value problem is a complex one. As a result, codes of ethics become too specific and elaborate, or so general that they have little usefulness as guides. Among physicians, judgments about ethical practice or malpractice, beyond those criteria defined by the Hippocratic oath, law, and formal professional statements, are based on what is accepted practice within a given geographical area.

Value problems therefore need to be talked through and the many facets of each problem examined. This need is especially imperative for young men who are relatively new to their work. Unless the conflicts are openly recognized as such and are discussed, under pressure from his superego the man is likely to feel angry with himself and with his organization. Resentment is a useless experience. The energy should go into doing the job itself.

CAUTIONS

It is easy to become impatient with young people if they do not see things as clearly as you see them. It is also easy to spend hours of thought on this kind of a problem. You must avoid these traps. If a few opportunities to talk beyond ordinary supervisory periods are not enough to help the man cope with his problem, then the problem is too complex for a layman.

You must be careful not to assume that the problem is strictly within the man. That means you should consider what the organization may be doing to accentuate the problem. It may be demanding too much allegiance and identification. It may stimulate certain value conflicts. It may cut off opportunities to grow or to use more of the man's capacities. For example, Drucker[13] reports that Sears, Roebuck assigned one incoming group of young men to its mail order warehouses and a comparable group to its retail stores. Five years later those in the stores had moved ahead in the organization. Some in the warehouses had left; those who had not left had made little progress, compared to those in the stores. In the stores, the men had opportunities to use much more of themselves. The two environments in the same company, which incidentally was trying hard to do its best for its people, were significantly different in their treatment of identity problems.

CHAPTER 12

Advancement Problems

THE TRANSITION FROM BEING AN EMPLOYEE TO BEING A supervisor, at whatever level in the hierarchy this occurs, is probably the single most important, psychological transition in a man's career. In the army it is said that a man feels more proud of his promotion from private to private first class than of any other promotion that may occur.

When a man is no one's superior, he has only the hierarchy above him to deal with. He does, of course, have to work with his colleagues or peers. When he becomes a supervisor or a manager, he acquires power over others. With power, he also acquires expectations on the part of subordinates about how he will use that power. The attitudes toward people who have power, which are developed in the family, are carried over into the work situation. Repeated surveys indicate that supervisors are expected to play a psychological role in the work situation much like that of the father in the family. The supervisor must treat his subordinates fairly, give them recognition, represent them to higher management, help them with their work (and sometimes personal) problems.[14]

The "father figure" aspects of being a superior are complicated by the composition of the group to be supervised. It is always difficult to assume such a role if a person has to supervise those who formerly were his associates, and it is even more difficult if his subordinates are obviously older than he. In both cases, the subordinates will keep testing to find out if the new superior will in fact be a leader, or whether, motivated by his own guilt feelings for having become more powerful than the others, he will see his exercise of authority as unduly aggressive. The former colleagues are likely to feel that he is like a "brother" and therefore has no business playing "father." The older subordinates are likely to feel that such a "son" has no business directing them. The new superior often shares some of the same feelings, but is usually embarrassed to say so. Most continue to struggle alone with this problems, for rarely do management development courses deal with them.

The new supervisor or manager has not only a higher level to deal with, he also has a lower one. Thereafter, no matter how high he rises, he must take both forces into account. Rarely, however, is he prepared for the psychological expectations that he will encounter from both. Usually he assumes that he is the same person he always was, unaware of how people's perceptions of him have changed as his power increased. And there is no escape from his position as long as he continues to have power.

The anxiety that arises out of the changed psychological position in which the new manager is likely to find himself should be anticipated and dealt with by his superiors. Part of the preparation of every new supervisor or manager should be a firm grounding about the psychological importance to other people of his new position and a full understanding of the many different ways he will now appear to those beneath him.

Anyone who becomes a supervisor or manager must learn his subordinates' reaction to his leadership. Without such a reaction, he cannot know how he is doing or what he should do differently. He must also learn that psychological data are as important to him as production, marketing, financial, and other data. Therefore he will require preparation in the basics of human behavior. Without such preparation, he will more likely try to "sell" people or manipulate them rather than try to motivate them. Manipulation ultimately fails, leaving anger in its wake. The difference between the two is significant. As used here, manipulation means persuading the other person to do what one wants him to do, regardless of the man's own personal interests. Motivation, by contrast, means learning what people want out of their work lives and finding ways in which their needs and the organization's needs can be met through joint effort.

It is a truism that everyone regards himself as a psychologist. Every self-respecting executive will say that he knows people. As a matter of fact, what most managers think they know about people is more often wrong than right, a point that Douglas McGregor[15] and others have made at great length.

If you were to manage a farm, probably you would write to the Department of Agriculture for all kinds of pamphlets on how to raise livestock and crops. When it comes to assuming responsibility for managing people, few managers see the need to study the vast body of experimental and clinical information concerning human motivation. The result is that a new supervisor's job is often a painful one—literally. As indicated in Chapter 9, it has been reported that there is a higher incidence of ulcers among first-level supervision than in any other position in the managerial hierarchy.

You will need to provide not only considerable factual

psychological knowledge, but also consistent support for the newly made supervisor or manager. At the time when he will be least skilled as a leader, he will require the strongest help. Learning to become a leader is in some ways like learning to ski. A man will stumble many times before he learns to ski. No support can prevent the falls, but a steadying hand can make the whole process considerably less painful.

FURTHER ADVANCEMENT

Promotion not infrequently brings people face to face with their own limitations. Some do not want to be promoted at all. Others would just as soon stop their upward climb at some given point, knowing that they cannot or do not want to assume increasing responsibility. In business circles, there is already a layman's diagnostic term, "promotion neurosis," for people who fail after promotion. Yet, many executives simply cannot understand the human limitations that bring about such feelings. They assume that everyone should want to be promoted and should welcome the opportunity for increased responsibility and income. When a man indicates that he has doubts about taking on increased responsibility, or if he declines promotion, his superiors tend to be disappointed and angry with him. "You don't have to move up in this company if you don't want to," they often say. In the next breath they add that the man who refuses promotion a second time is likely to be bypassed in the future.

A man may decline promotion for many reasons. Some feel quite realistically that they have all they want both psychologically and materially and see no advantage to them in taking on a bigger job. Others know they do not have the skills or talents for the larger job. Still others are limited by their own superegos: They may not have enough confidence in themselves, or unconsciously they may feel that they do not deserve the better position and higher income. For some, promotion may mean loss of previous supports for dependent needs and increasing the risk of failure. Whatever the reasons, there is little point in pushing them. In such instances, you would do better to accept a man's own definitions of his limitations. To push him against his better judgment may well cause difficulties.

If you are responsible for the promotion of others, you should not take it for granted that even those who show promise will be ready for advancement when it comes. You should clearly define the anticipated new responsibilities, make it possible for the candidate to think through the implications of the new position and to decline gracefully if he wishes. This is sometimes not easy for a man to do with equanimity, particularly if the senior executive has spent considerable time and effort training him for more responsibility. Nor will the senior be happy if he has counted on his subordinate to fill an important gap in the hierarchy. But it will be easier for the senior man to live with his disappointment than for both the subordinate and the organization to pay the price for the subordinate's later inadequate performance. The point of promotion is probably the most critical point for a "Dutch uncle" talk if frankness and exposure of a man's feelings are safe in that company. If it is not safe to talk freely, some men will give in to the pressure and assume the new responsibilities, regardless of whether they feel capable.

Other men will not discover until they have been promoted that they have made a mistake. Promotion for Bob Lyons, for example, took him away from the personal activity he needed so badly. Once a man is promoted, it is then difficult to bow out gracefully unless specific trial periods can be set up to try out new jobs. Few companies have such trial arrangements. In some companies, try-outs may not be feasible. Other companies may not put men in new posts until the last possible minute, thus making a trial impossible. But those companies that have had too much executive failure might think of such a possibility.

When a man is promoted, he is usually in a situation quite different from the one he left. Even if he stays in the same physical place, his newly acquired power changes his psychological situation. When there are changes in position and expectation, increased support from superiors during the initial weeks in the new job will help relieve the stress of the change. This can take the form of more frequent reporting and discussion meetings, formally scheduled, so that the newly promoted man will have ample opportunity to talk over his new problems. If the initiative is left to him to seek out his superiors, he is unlikely to do so, feeling that to ask for help is a sign of weakness. Of course he can be left to sink or swim, but that is a high-cost method of learning. Not many executives want to be responsible for drowning a man in his own career.

ATTITUDES TOWARD ADVANCEMENT

Rational consideration of advancement is made more difficult by contemporary social attitudes in business and government. The military and the U.S. Department of State, for example, both operate on the principle of "up or out." That is, if a man is not recommended for promotion within a certain period of time, he must leave the service. Such a policy, though perhaps useful in some ways, constitutes a constant pressure to assume more responsibility and is intolerant of human weakness. As a result, a man must cover up his inadequacies and sometimes pretend a level of confidence and capacity he does not have. This often leaves him feeling guilty and deprives him of the support he might have had from his superiors, with which he might have done a more satisfactory job.

Much the same pressure exists in large business organizations. There is a distinct tendency to look upon a man who either has not been promoted regularly, or who does not want promotion, as having failed. In one major American business, there are two kinds of executives, according to company folklore: the "jets," those who have moved quickly through the ranks; and the "popos," who are pushed out and passed over.

Objectively, it is ridiculous to think that a man is a failure because he has not attained a certain position in an organizational hierarchy. Few people, however, can be so objective in the face of strong social pressure. Many therefore live with unreasonable feelings of inadequacy. These feelings take their toll in chronic resentment, which takes the form of anger with oneself and with the company, sapping energy that might more usefully be directed to the job. As long as rewards are scaled in terms of administrative position rather than job competence, the pyramidal structure of administration makes it inevitable that although some will achieve success, many more will feel that they have failed.

A young executive rarely moves rapidly through the hierarchy without also having mixed feelings about his success. While he may be pleased with himself and his progress, he usually also has doubts and guilt feelings. He knows that there are many older and wiser heads in the organization than his. He knows also of the jealousy and resentment that follow his progress and of the disappointment that others must experience because of his success. He is all too keenly aware of his inexperience and of the heavy dependence of his superiors upon him. He does not dare fail. Rarely can he express his feelings about his new job with his superiors, for they have put a halo around him and left him to his own supposedly adequate devices. Frequently he tries to atone for his advancement by appeasing those who have been by-passed, which only increases their anger without relieving his guilt feelings. Here is a case in point:

Bill Lewis, now fifty-seven, has been a branch manager for the subsidiary of a national organization for
• twelve years. He had had a twenty-eight-year successful record within the subsidiary and has turned down opportunities in other subsidiaries, anticipating that he might become president of the one in which he had done so well. When the presidency became vacant, a younger branch manager with fifteen years of experience was appointed because the board thought Lewis lacked some of the qualities a president would need. The new man, Tom White, felt Lewis' resentment and repeatedly asked himself how he could obtain Lewis' confidence and co-operation. From time to time he would visit Lewis. Each time he would tell Lewis how hard the president's job was and how lucky Lewis was not to have it. He could not understand why Lewis was becoming more resentful despite his efforts to be friendly with Lewis. He could not see that his own guilt feelings for having "taken" Lewis' job made him angry with both himself and Lewis. As a result, he kept prodding Lewis, without being conscious of the attacking nature of his comments. Of course Lewis rejected him even more.

When you promote a younger man over others who are older and more experienced, you should help him recognize that he will have doubts and perhaps guilt feelings. These are not unusual. However, he is the new superior. He will have to accept that fact and so will his subordinates. He has responsibilities to his superiors and his men have responsibilities toward him. Both will have to fulfill their respective responsibilites; he will have to hold them to theirs, as you will hold him to his. His promotion is a fact of life with which both parties will have to live. The sooner they do so the better. Such a firm and realistic position will do much to ease the anxiety and insecurity the older men have about the new superior and the new superior has about himself. Of course, as indicated earlier, they will test him to see if he really means what he says. If they find that he is not consistent, which he may not be if your own support is inconsistent, then there will be panic and anarchy in the work group.

ISOLATION

Perhaps the most common negative feeling that accompanies promotion is the increasing feeling of isolation. Certainly, no feeling is more frequently expressed among any group of presidents. The old army saying that the commanding officer is the loneliest man on the post is equally true in business circles. The many perquisites that accompany increasing stature do not replace the lost personal contacts in which opinions and ideas were freely exchanged.

In addition to exchanging opinions and ideas in our everyday relationships, we have interdependent experiences with people. We exchange invitations and help with each other, but we have little formal responsibility for each other. When a man becomes someone else's superior, he assumes some degree of responsibility for the other. Many men have difficulty accepting the dependent needs of others, whether as employers or fathers; this is one reason for avoiding promotion. Also, having power over others is to lose the camaraderie of equals, being "one of the boys." Some do not want to give up that source of affection. And some have difficulty accepting themselves as persons who have power over others.

Clarence Randall, retired chairman of Inland Steel, has pointed out[16] that, "Responsibility breeds isolation. . . . After an executive reaches the very top, he is seldom seen in public and seldom heard. He becomes a myth." Randall noted that the young executive was in constant touch with others when he lived closely with neighbors whose work ranged over many occupations. But when the executive began to move up, his growing exclusiveness deprived him of the opportunity to be exposed to varying opinions. He lived in a more exclusive area, more distant from the neighbors, and no longer rode the commuter trains or shared rides. As a result, he became increasingly out of touch with crosscurrents around him and with those who might differ with him. Randall advised executives to expose themselves to the questions of newspapermen and students, to break out of their isolated and protected social cocoons, and to become involved directly with the complex world around them.

An executive becomes necessarily more aloof than he was as a colleague because he cannot express his doubts or misgivings lest he panic his subordinates. Again the parallel between his position and that of the father in the family is evident. Nor can he get undistorted information from subordinates because the traditional staff organizational pattern on which most business organizations are modeled fosters dependency and self-protection. Each person at every point in the hierarchy is dependent upon the person above him for appraisal, promotion, and even for holding his job.

Each must cope with the concept of control implied in the hierarchical system. To do that, he does his best to protect himself from those below who would unseat him, and from those above who decide his occupational destiny.

The higher the executive goes, the more distorted are the perceptions of him from below. He is viewed as both omnipotent and inadequate. His inability to know all that is happening to them, to rectify injustices, and to correct the mistakes makes it possible to criticize him because he does not demonstrate omnipotence. No one is more conscious than he that not only does he miss much that is going on in his organization, but also that he is a long way from being omnipotent.

To add to his isolation, he is fed a steady diet of information in the popular management journals designed to fit his biases, particularly when it comes to information about unions and the labor movement. For example, a widely read management magazine published a story on the AFL-CIO Community Services Committee. The story was accurate in all details, except that the publication could not be satisfied with a factually accurate story. It devoted a good part of the introduction of the article to telling the executive reader that this activity of the unions was another device to win away the loyalty of the employees from management. Actually, nothing in the labor movement could be further from labor-management conflict, for this arm of the labor movement is devoted to developing and maintaining labor support for community and voluntary health agencies. It is little comfort to the executive to know that his labor counterpart often gets slanted information about him.

The executive is often manipulated by the professional staffs of management service organizations such as Chambers of Commerce, Associations of Manufacturers, and similar groups. These men so often devote themselves to crying "wolf" and providing information to support the danger cry, that the executive who depends on them for information is on tenuous ground. To compensate for such distortion, the executive should always ask what any informant wants him to believe, and he should allow for the biases of the informant. Unfortunately, most executives do not have sufficient skepticism in this area.

Thomas J. Watson points out that it is not enough for management to be against new ideas; it must itself provide ideas for progress.[17] Yet, the traditional professional spokesmen for management historically have had the executive in an "agin" position. That is, management was opposed to the abolition of child labor and the enactment of social security. It offered no positive efforts to deal with these problems. Little wonder that an executive finds that his employees do not share his views and that he is isolated from them.

The place to begin dealing with the problem of isolation from the men who report to you is in your relationship to them. The principle on which you act is that the ego can deal with reality best if it has the clearest possible picture of reality with a minimum of rationalization and projection. In terms of your own behavior, this means that you should make it possible for those who report to you to think critically for themselves, to give you their views of leadership behavior, and to talk freely with you about their ideas and feelings. This cannot be done if you do not genuinely want to hear them, for they will realize that you do not want to listen. One company president said plaintively, "I don't know what's the matter with my top management group. We have a staff meeting every Monday morning. I tell them what I think. Then I ask them what they think. And nobody says anything." His method of telling them first what he thought was only one way of unconsciously stating that he did not want to hear them.

If you can support your own subordinates so they can speak freely with you, then they will have less need to be defensive. In turn, they have an easier time of it with their subordinates, who also can report more freely.

As part of the reporting process, you can and should ask of those who report to you how their people are thinking and feeling about the work situation. You must recognize that your subordinates often will not communicate because they will not want to bother you with what seem to be trivia. They will go to some lengths to protect you. Both will cut you off from information you might want to have. You will therefore have to make it clear you want information and will protect yourself. The information you require demands that they report first-hand conversations. Without first-hand contact with their subordinates, the latter can get no sense of esteem from superiors nor any recognition that their work has been noticed.

Probably the most frequent comment to be heard in managerial ranks is, "I don't know where I stand." This does not mean that the man who says it has not been appraised or critically evaluated. Usually it means that he has no idea how he is regarded by his superiors, despite appraisal. Regard and esteem are communicated by frequent personal contacts. Without such contacts, a man has only his own fantasies to go on. People who are not altogether satisfied that they are doing as well as they should, and those who are moving upward, are not likely to be satisfied at various positions along the way, are more likely than others to need frequent reassurances. Formal appraisals are too far apart chronologically to serve this need, and too often they are impersonal.

The leader who tries to support the growth of people in their jobs will find that he has far fewer problems of getting accurate information. His subordinates will recognize that he is working on their behalf and will not need to defend themselves against him. They can more freely report their mistakes if these become the bases for further learning rather than weapons later to be used against them. They need not pretend a competence they do not feel if the leader permits them to talk over their weak points and helps them work out ways of dealing more effectively with their shortcomings. Without such an atmosphere, the leader is in the position of picking out their weaknesses himself, and then criticizing them. When a man thus feels he must defend himself, he is not in a favorable psychological position for learning.

It is easy for any manager to be oppressed with paper work and to become bound to his immediate tasks. His own superior—you—should not let him isolate himself in this way. Nor should you accept a different form of isolation, the mere mouthing of clichés from the management literature. For example, often a top manager has resolved certain problems of relationships with unions and has accepted the fact that unions are here to stay. But a few levels below, his subordinates speak as if they were still living in the 1930s and firmly believe they are reflecting their superior's attitudes.

SHIFTS IN JOB DEMANDS

Another major psychological problem for the advancing executive is the often required shift in activity and perspective. When a man enters a business organization, usually he does so because he wants to compete in the business world. If he advances, he does so because presumably his performance has been better than someone else's. He himself *does* something. But as he moves up the hierarchy, he is required to shift from direct competition to delegating responsibility and authority and to fostering the competitive ability of the particular group he heads.

This means that he must renounce much of his own activity and facilitate the work of others. It also means that he is frequently less dependent upon his own efforts and more dependent upon those of his subordinates. To be more dependent on others is also to be more vulnerable, for the executive is held accountable for the errors and failures of those who report to him.

It is not easy to change from doing something oneself to facilitating and supervising the work of others. Many executives, particularly those who have moved from sales or production to administration, long for the direct relationship with customers or the direct involvement with production. Some cannot give up the involvement and continue to intrude into the work of their subordinates. There is a shopworn cliché in management circles that many a good salesman has been turned into a poor sales manager.

Furthermore, to be dependent upon subordinates and to have to help them assume increasing responsibilities, reawakens old conflicts about dependency and rivalry. Many an executive, in the privacy of his own thoughts, will admit to himself that he really does not want to help others advance. The editor of a national magazine expressed this quite frankly in the confines of his own office. Discussing this problem, he said, "I don't think I have ever helped anyone on my staff. I wouldn't dare. They might take my job."

The man who chooses to move up the executive ladder should recognize that leadership is an act of renunciation. He will have to give up some of his activities and make it possible for others to do them. This may mean some conflict with his image of himself, a conflict that is particularly acute for researchers who become managers of research laboratories and salesmen who become sales managers.

Nevertheless, if the leader is to do his job in an organization, he must, with his subordinates, define their mutual responsibilities. Together they will have to set their joint goals. Then it is his task to give support, to facilitate getting the job done. In the process of his relationships with his subordinates, centered on the job to be done, he also makes it possible for them to talk with him about their job problems. Taken together, these supportive activities help to develop people's capabilities. And that is his major function if his primary concern is with the survival of the organization.

Another consequence of advancement is a greater demand for community leadership. The more power an executive acquires, the more he is expected to use that power in the interest of the community. United Fund drives, voluntary health and service agencies, educational and church institutions, all demand his leadership and leverage. Without it, they cannot succeed. Often the executive undertakes such tasks unwillingly and as obligations. They constitute an added burden when he already feels burdened by his business obligations. He frequently feels poorly contained irritation at the demands, but dares not show his resentment publicly lest he jeopardize his company's community relations.

The most difficult part of advancement, at least for some men, is that the gratification is short-lived. The sense of achievement, if it is tied primarily to promotions, comes to a halt when the man has either reached the top or has gone as far as he can. Without intrinsic satisfaction from the work itself, no achievement is fully satisfying.

In practice, with regard to advancement in executive

ranks, a man ought to have a reasonably clear picture of what advancement means to him. Does he want it because it is a better use of his capabilities and abilities or because of the myth that nonadvancement means he is a failure? As Thurber once put it, "All men should learn before they die, what they are running to and from and why."

If a man seeks advancement because of someone else's values or in order to enhance himself in the eyes of others, or if he is trying to prove something to himself, he is likely to find that his achievements will not bring him the satisfactions he seeks. If, however, advancement means opportunity for greater creativity or contribution, that is another story. In either case, though, he should try to evaluate the limits of his skills and capabilities. Then, out of fairness to himself and the organization he serves, he can anticipate—and often avoid—stress. A careful review of his own job history, in which he seeks out those aspects of his work that have given him satisfaction and those that has posed difficulties, becomes a good base line for evaluating the relative merits of other opportunities that are offered to him. Such considerations raised by an interested superior makes them acceptable to the younger executive. More serious thought about the meaning of promotion may well mean fewer promotion failures and the emotional pain that goes with them.

An engineer who had been a very successful plant manager had so much difficulty with the executive vice-president of his company that he finally resigned. As he analyzed his experience, he came to recognize that though he did very well as a plant manager, and had done equally well in each preceding job he had had, he could not work comfortably in a loosely structured situation. Without firm, consistent support from his superiors, he had too much tension in his job, at whatever level he had operated. Because he had been a successful plant manager, he was offered many similar positions. His friends could not understand why he turned each of them down and instead sought a more limited job.

A man may have difficulty examining his motives by himself. It is understandable that he may not want to talk about them even to the most supportive kind of a superior. He would find it helpful, therefore, to have someone to whom he could talk freely. A wise superior will suggest that he might wish to talk with someone else. Management consultants often serve just such a function. Medical officers in the military service, because they are outside the usual chain of command, are also called upon for the same purpose.

The confidant need not be a professional person. A man is fortunate if he can talk to his wife. A good friend, family doctor, or pastor—anyone who can be trusted to listen and retain a confidence—can serve in this capacity. If, however, a man finds that certain problems related to his own feelings or behavior come up repeatedly in these discussions and are not resolved by talking about them, then it is time to consult a professional about them. In these days there are enough clinical psychologists and psychiatrists available so that a person need not continue to suffer the effects of unresolved personal problems without trying to do something about them. A man's inability to formulate reasonable goals for himself, to find satisfactions in his promotions, or the work related to them is an example.

This discussion necessarily leaves out the pleasures, rewards, and achievements of advancement. In that sense, it is one-sided. But it is not meant to minimize leadership. To assume increasing responsibility for leadership and to discharge it effectively is to make an extremely important social contribution. The abilities inherent in groups of people remain merely potential until effective leadership mobilizes and guides them. Our concern, therefore, is with increasing leadership effectiveness by seeking to recognize and alleviate some of the emotional factors that may retard its development.

CHAPTER 13

Family Problems

WHEN A MAN COMES TO AN ORGANIZATION, HE IS LIKELY TO be a family man. The organization takes little official notice of that fact. Both the man and the organization rightfully feel it is his business. Yet, if the man is in managerial ranks, before he advances very far in some companies or governmental units, his wife will be judged just as he is being judged. If the assignment in question is overseas, then the evaluation of the wife is likely to be more open and direct. Overseas failure, often due to the wife's inability to adjust to the foreign culture, is too expensive to be treated lightly. If the assignment is a domestic one, evaluation of the wife is likely to be much more subtle and informal.

Some will object that it is unfair to evaluate a man's wife. *He,* not she, is being employed. As a matter of fact, when a man has a responsible leadership post, for all practical purposes both he and his wife are employed. This is an old story in the military and the ministry. It is not openly recognized or accepted in industry. There are many ways a wife can use her husband's power position, which automatically gives her status in a community. How she chooses to do so

185

can enhance his career and the fortunes of the organization, or bring discredit on both. Management has no choice but to think of the effect of the wife's behavior on its community relations.

The problem is not that the organization intrudes into family relationships. Rather, that it is unaware that its subtle intrusions may be destructive, and of other ways in which it might intrude which could be supportive without being paternalistic. The organization that makes a considerable investment in a potential manager should be aware of how his family may inadvertently impair its investment, what other events might affect its stake in the man, and what might be done to ease some of the stresses.

The pursuit of many careers, managerial or otherwise, often poses a question for both husband and wife before a marriage is very far along. That question is sometimes given a half-facetious twist: To whom are you married, the wife or the career? But humor does not really ease the dilemma.

One common starting point for a conflict between family and career is the point of first psychological separation of husband and wife. If both are working, they are separated physically during the day, but that does not seem to be much of a problem. They share their experiences in the evening. When the couple begins to have children, however, often the young wife feels bound to her home during the day. She has responsibilities for the children, which make it difficult for her to have time and energy to share experiences with her husband. With these responsibilities, her daily life tends to be more circumscribed and constricted than it was before. She often feels her world to be bounded by Pooh Corner and the Mulberry Bush, as a series of *New York Times* ads once put it. Sometimes she is resentful toward her husband because she feels him to be responsible for her burdens and because, in her view, he has freedom which she does not have. While she eats the children's unfinished peanut butter sandwiches for lunch, ferries them from lessons to doctors, and serves as a Den mother, and works for the PTA, her husband is more likely to be having business lunches and traveling cross-country on company missions. Furthermore, he is in touch with a wide range of people, tackling important business problems, and otherwise expanding his personal sphere of activity.

Although this picture is something of a caricature, many wives of executives see it as not very unlike their everyday experiences. From the moment the husband and wife begin to live in separate worlds, they run the danger of the separation growing ever wider.

There are many different kinds of separation, and each has its own mechanism. If the husband's job provides him with stimulation and personal growth and his wife does not keep up with him, she will soon be left behind psychologically if not literally. Mrs. Oliver Wendell Holmes was reported to have remarked to Teddy Roosevelt, "Washington is a place of many brilliant men and the girls they married when they were very young."

There is a reverse twist to differential rates of growth. Some men become so preoccupied with their specialty that they are illiterate in everything else. Some leave all the responsibility for community activities to their wives. If, in both instances, the wives move ahead, not only are they soon more knowledgeable than their husbands, but also, more importantly, the lack of knowledge of the husband often leads to resentment. Some working women quit their jobs because they sense the rising hostility of their husbands.

The arrival of children often becomes a device of separation. Men, despite their age, can resent losing attention and affection because their wives must give more attention to the children and are therefore more fatigued. Sometimes the wife's fatigue is a product of her efforts to repress her unconscious hostility toward her husband if she sees him as the cause of her burdens of motherhood and her more constricted life. "I made up my mind before I married," said one mother of four, "that I would be so attentive to my husband that he would never have time to think of another woman. But by the end of the day I'm exhausted and I can't live up to my intentions."

A marriage is the most intimate of all partnerships. Its survival requires the development of common bonds and mutual experiences. Particularly during the child rearing period, when the two partners are likely to be preoccupied with their separate responsibilities, special effort is necessary to maintain the ties. Young people may not be aware that they are being estranged, yet they may sense their increasing resentment of each other. The resulting anger of the husband may be displaced at work or reflect itself in symptoms. When job performance is affected, then the superior may be able to point out the stress points of this particular period and the need to work toward relieving them.

The superior is in a difficult position if the organization is contributing to the separation. It often does so in three important ways:

1. *When the Company Makes Inordinate Time Demands.* In one major American corporation, executives go to work before the hourly workers arrive in the morning, and the lights burn every night. When some of the young executives were asked whether their work actually required so much time, they said the work itself did not. But no one wanted to be thought less eager than the next man. And the superiors, to justify themselves to higher management, would

frequently call staff meetings at 6:30 P.M. The young executives in this situation are pawns in a vast confidence game. They and the company may be playing "make believe" with each other, but no one is deceiving the wives and children.

An interesting sidelight to this situation followed an executive's suicide in this organization. When one of the vice-presidents was asked if the company was not concerned about the suicide and about the possible stresses in the work situation which might have contributed to it, he shrugged his shoulders. They had executives ready to take the places of others at all levels, the vice-president said, and many men were competing for higher positions. If some fell by the wayside, that was too bad. They should not have entered such a competitive business in the first place. The same company, in its national advertising, makes a point of telling the public how important its employees are in its business. Apparently executives are not regarded in that organization as employees.

2. *When the Company Permits the Man to Sacrifice His Family to the Organization.* Young men who are determined to move up in the executive hierarchy often do so by sacrificing their families. One young district sales manager for an office equipment manufacturer said quite bluntly, "I'm going to go up in this company and nothing is going to stop me." One of the senior executives of the company, in another comment, made it clear that though his company cherished motherhood and abhorred sin, the men who got ahead in that organization were those who put the company first.

This fact is not lost on others in the community. Between the sessions of a seminar in an East Coast community, a volunteer in the local mental health association took a company medical director to task. "You know," she said angrily, "when a woman marries a man who works for the Company, the marriage contract ought to read, 'I, Mary, take thee, John, and the Company, to be my lawful wedded spouse. . . .' I've seen these women left all alone to shift for themselves and their children while their husbands are gone for weeks at a time for the greater glory of the Company."

Those young men who decide that they will pursue their career goals single-mindedly often do so on the assumption that after they reach their goals, they will then relax and enjoy their families. More often than not, this turns out to be a painful pipe dream. While they are so busy with their careers, their wives and families learn to live without them and go their own ways. Those who become successful are often left with feelings of guilt and the question, "What did I work for?" In addition, if they have not been enjoying their family relationships all along, they can hardly begin to do so when they are past middle age.

Much of the time, a young man and his wife know that to work for success in a competitive culture will frequently require sacrifices. Women's magazines devote many articles to this problem, and the men have heard their share of sermons about the sacrifices they make. However, the mechanism of denial is wondrously efficient—people hear the words, but do not take them personally. If the company is to deal with this problem, it must do so in two ways. The company must avoid making unnecessary demands that would interfere with family life. Also, superiors must repeatedly call attention to the kind of job behavior that is likely to precipitate family difficulty. Chronic conflict between husband and wife can have an important bearing on the man's progress, and he should know that his superiors are not interested in buying rapid progress at the possible cost of his being bogged down later.

3. *When the Company Moves People Rapidly and Arbitrarily.* One of the critical problems for a family is having to move from one community to another to serve the needs of the business. One-fifth of all the families in the United States move each year. Three-fourths of all the people who move in any one year are members of large business or governmental organizations. Some young executives move almost every year. (And some have never discussed any move with their wives.)

The children of many of today's executives, and of some government officials, will never know the hometown as their parents knew it. They have moved too many times. Instead of a hometown, the organization becomes the consistent orienting point. Often a young man enters an organization before he marries and remains with it after his grandchildren are grown. He may move many places, but always with the same ties to the organization. It becomes the single continuous thread of his life. But most of the time it is a thread for the man only. His wife and children have to adapt many times.

It is a tribute to human flexibility that wives and children adapt as well as they do. But it is often difficult for the wife to establish new friends and re-establish old, comfortable modes of living. One phenomenon, which has been observed but not yet statistically validated, is the frequency with which accidental pregnancy occurs shortly after the wife learns her family has to move. This, it seems, is an unconscious restitutive mechanism by which the lost home or community is replaced and is also a way to control the new situation. A woman gets much more consideration from her husband and others when she is pregnant. Pregnancy further serves as a rationale for limiting participation in the new community except on one's own terms. Preoccupied with an infant, a woman can, without being criticized, adapt at her own pace. In some cases, it can also be a way of striking back at the husband and of keeping him at a distance from her.

Often it is not easy for children to give up their friends and to break into new social circles. This seems to be particularly true in high school. Separation from the familiar is always a distressing experience. It is even more so when it occurs repeatedly and to children who are trying to establish stable points in their lives as reference points for growing up.

One of the penalties of frequent movement is the likelihood of limiting one's investment in other people and activities. If people feel they are likely to be moving soon after they enter a community, then their ties to that community probably will be shallow and tenuous. There is no point in establishing close friendships or getting involved in community enterprises if painful separation will soon follow. Thus the ego is deprived of some of its possible sources of gratification.

A State Department official, discussing this problem, said that he tried not to make close friendships in his overseas assignments because it hurt too much to leave friends. His solution was to try to maintain his friendships in his hometown and renew them between tours of overseas duty. But this solution depended on the permanence of his friends in that community, and that in itself was questionable.

One of the frequent results of the psychological as well as physical separation of husband and wife is marital infidelity. Separation because of the requirements of the business, the need to entertain customers, and the instability that results from frequent moving, all contribute to this problem. No one knows what the emotional price is in terms of impaired relationships between husband and wife or of the guilt feelings that result from "climbing the fence," as it is called. The problem is sufficiently widespread, however, that whenever the question is broached in executive groups, the response is either a dead silence or an angry defensiveness.

How can an executive act to anticipate some of these problems and to counteract some of their potential stress?

1. *In training and orientation programs for management trainees, time should be devoted to anticipating and discussing these problems.* Management development means preparing men for better problem solving and more effective managerial roles. Wiser problem solving at home may relieve the man of considerable stress on the job and leave him with more energy for self-development. In addition, it is important for management to set the tone early that problems are best dealt with and resolved, not covered over and contained. This holds for family problems as well as business problems.

2. *When a man has difficulty on the job and relates it to marital problems, if he talks about it with a more senior executive, the latter should encourage him to discuss the problem with his wife.* While this may seem to be a banal suggestion, the fact is that when people begin to differ, they tend to withdraw from each other. They may then go through the motions of conversation, but also make great efforts to avoid painful conflict and therefore do not really communicate. Sometimes they have learned not to communicate so well that it takes a third party to help them do so. That third party, however, should *not* be the executive. If they cannot resolve their problem by themselves, then suggest that they get professional help. No problem is more

touchy to deal with than a conflict between husband and wife, and no problem harder to avoid, since both partners seek allies. Besides, beyond seeing that the requirements of the job are met and listening long enough to know that he has to refer the couple for help, the superior has no business knowing the personal details of employees' lives. Both he and they will be much better off if he does not know.

3. *Review the time demands of the job.* Does it really require all the time devoted to it, or is the employee just doing what he thinks is expected of him? Is excess time on the job something for which the organization might later pay by losing a good man? Is it a way of evading a family problem? Is the organization getting quantity of time rather than quality of work? Is someone exploiting men by inordinate demands? If the executive finds that he gets negative answers to these questions, then he should ask: What really is expected and how will it be measured or judged?

4. *Consider how people are moved.* Is it done precipitously? Has the anticipated move been cleared with the wife, and has she had an opportunity to learn and talk about the problems she might run into in the new community? Does she feel that she is being exploited? Has the company taken the trouble to organize a packet of materials husband and wife might read to better prepare themselves and their children for the move? Two such articles are: "Families on the Move," by Dr. Robert E. Switzer in the *Menninger Quarterly,* Summer, 1961, and "Children Move to a New Home," by Dr. Lois B. Murphy in the same publication, Spring, 1962. There are others as well.

The problems of moving might also be a part of indoctrination, particularly because moves occur most frequently among young men. Academic courses offer no preparation for the personal problems related to their work. They will not know how to help their wives and children adapt, nor of the particular importance of maintaining the integrity of the family.

5. *Make it clear that you are not interfering in a man's personal life, but you do have a stake in his mental health and his continuing progress in your organization.* You therefore want him to know what problems he is likely to encounter during the course of his career, both in and out of the company, and ways in which he might cope with them. Two matters in particular need his constant attention: his marriage and his enjoyment of life. The first matter requires treating the wife consistently in ways that communicate love, interest, and need. It means also keeping differences out in the open where both parties can work at resolving them. The second matter involves recognizing that a person who gets all his satisfactions from one area of his life, whether it is his business or something else, suffers severe loss if anything happens to deprive him of that satisfaction. With a wide range of gratifications from which to draw stimulation and affection, the ego has the flexibility to cope with stress situations that deprive a person of one or another of his sources of support.

It has been said inaccurately that 95 per cent of all emotional problems on the job result from problems at home. Many executives, believing this, hold it to be a man's own responsibility to resolve those problems. As has been observed, the problems of home and job are often interrelated, for those that arise in one sphere will infect the other. Thus, help that is provided in one sphere can carry over into the other. Just as the interest and support of a man's wife frequently makes it possible for him to cope more effectively with job crises, so similar help from the organization makes it possible to cope more effectively with family crises. In both spheres, the man's responsibility remains his own, but he is not alone in facing it.

Sometimes it is just as difficult for a husband and wife to put this concept into practice as it is for the executive to do so in his relationships with his subordinates. A man may perceive his wife's interest as interference. He may feel less of a man for talking over problems with his wife. Some do not even want their wives to know how much money they make. The wife, in turn, may use her husband's confidence in her as a way of manipulating him to gratify her own power needs.

Some people, of course, are unable to sustain their marriages for many different reasons. It is neither the responsibility nor to the interest of the organization to exert pressure one way or the other. Such problems should be taken to a professional. That they exist should not deter the executive from providing organizational support to the strength of family whenever and however possible.

CHAPTER 14

Age Problems

UNTIL A MAN REACHES MIDDLE AGE, HE SEES HIS FUTURE AHEAD of him. A man in his forties knows that in all likelihood he has fewer years ahead of him than behind. If he has not already reached the pinnacles to which he aspired at twenty-one, the probabilities of reaching them grow less with increasing years. Usually, he has to settle for achievements that may be commendable in themselves but which invariably fall below his aspirations. Most men must accept the fact that they will remain in much the same position as they find themselves at middle age. They will have to live with the feeling that "This is it."

For many men, middle age poses no particular problems. It may be highly enjoyable. These men will be well established in their careers or businesses. The early years of struggle will be only memories. They will be able to look upon their achievements with pride and satisfaction. Some will have established themselves so well financially that their mortgages have been paid off and their financial responsibilities to their children have been met. Many men will be proud when their children go off to college or choose a career, satisfied with the job they have done as fathers, and basking in the reflected glory of their children's achievements. Often, such men will then turn their attention to public service; some will begin to travel or to undertake long-postponed activities. Those who have been wise enough to work at their marriages all along will find new depth in their relationships with their wives.

Yet other men find this period particularly painful. For such men there is no question that the middle-age transition period is a "change of life," even though there is no radical biochemical change as there is in women.

A man in this group, even if he is in good health, winces inwardly when his children refer to him as "old" and mean it. He is urged each winter to be cautious about shoveling snow lest he have a coronary. He also begins to experience a psychological desertion. Despite his pride and pleasure in his children's activities, they either are about to leave the family circle or have already left. They have their own adult lives to lead and their own families to rear.

Taken together, these changes make it apparent for a man that he is not what he used to be and that his course is inevitably a downward one.

This crisis of mid-life is a serious, often painful problem— to the men who are afflicted, to their families, and to their business associates and executives. It creates, in turn, other problems for executives because they are responsible for the performance of the men whose work they must supervise. A wise superior, anticipating some of these problems, may help a subordinate identify them in time to avoid possible deterioration of work performance as well as personal pain.

For example, as was mentioned in the preceding chapter, some highly successful men decide early in their careers that they will put first things first, meaning career success. They work hard achieving success only to discover that what they have attained is only a part of what they really want. Here is one such case:

A man, in his late forties, owned three sizable companies. He was the son of poor farm parents; he had managed to get through high school and then went to work in the oil fields. The small company he worked for became highly successful, and he became its president at an early age. He expanded his holdings, bought the controlling interest in a bank, later added a medium-sized manufacturing company. Meanwhile, he had married, and his two children were away in school. He had determined early that he would make a success of himself, and when he had achieved his success, he would then "really live it up" and make up for his many sacrifices. Now he had success, but he could find no pleasure: He did not really know his children; they had little to say to him and he to them. They had long since learned they could not discuss their problems with him. His wife had her own interests. He did not know how to go about enjoying himself. As he looked back on his life, his achievements were, in his eyes, for nothing. The world saw him as a success; he saw himself as a failure.

MIDDLE-AGE THREATS

The middle-aged man begins to be more aware of death. In his early adult years, a man felt that death, barring accidents, was a long way off. He was familiar with happy events: He recognized the names of his friends in engagement, wedding, and birth announcements in the local newspaper. In middle age, he begins to recognize the names in the obituary column more frequently and to shake his head over the premature death of some of his friends.

His circle of friends narrows as he grows older. Along the way, his interests have changed and probably have become narrower. He tends less frequently to see those people who do not share his interests. By middle age, he finds himself most comfortable with a few old friends. His circle of friends becomes even smaller as death decreases their number. Yet he may be only dimly aware of this constriction, for he still sees many familiar faces.

Middle age is thus for many men a period of acute psychological loss. *Superiors should be fully aware of this factor or they may well misinterpret a man's behavior.* The losses are made even more painful by the recognition that there are aggressive rivals who threaten to dethrone them. In almost any field, younger men have acquired new skills and techniques with which they will ultimately outdo the older men. The older men fear to lose their self-respect if they admit that what they have been doing is no longer adequate. To accept the newer ways, for some, is to make that admission. If they do change, they admit the younger men are right. If they fail to change, they run the risk of seeing younger men move rapidly ahead of them. They are stimulated to defensive competition at the very time in their careers when competition would seem to offer the least rewards in the form of advancement and when they are already coping with severe psychological stresses.

Some withdraw from the competition. These are the men who, in terms of cultural conceptions of success, have reached a plateau. "We can't do anything to budge our middle-aged engineers," said the president of an engineering firm. "I don't know what gets into them, but they seem to stop at dead center." A college president made the same complaint about his faculty. "We give them early promotions to encourage them to produce," he said, "but it doesn't seem to do any good. They coast along comfortably in ruts and you can't force a man to be creative." Like a wounded animal who seeks the protection of its cave, a man in such a position may well build a psychological cocoon around himself.

Others become hostile to possible competitors and to superiors. In ways that are difficult to see, they may refuse to train younger men. They may use the younger men as flunkies, or criticize them harshly, all in the name of giving them good training. Hostility to the superior is more often expresesd passively in the failure to do what they are capable of doing.

The multiple psychological losses that combine to make some men feel that they are less manly than before may lead to impulsive behavior. Extramarital affairs that occur for the first time during this period may be viewed as efforts to hold onto one's masculinity and to regain the youthful experiences of romance and excitement. Such affairs are seldom psychologically rewarding. Instead, they often add guilt to other already pressing psychological problems.

The feeling of being less manly reawakens old conflicts about being dependent. As was noted in Chapter 1, given the long period of dependency on parents in our culture, everyone struggles with the wish to become independent versus the pleasures of remaining dependent. This is particularly the struggle of the adolescent. When a man becomes an adult, he asserts his independence, but in some ways everyone has to depend on others. When a man feels less adult, his dependent wishes come more to the surface. But, since he is in fact an adult, it is difficult for him to face such wishes.

Alcoholism is one way of attempting to cope with the conflict about dependency wishes. Some men, particularly those who have lost important sources of affection, or who are severely disappointed in themselves, may become depressed. Depression in response to these change-of-life stresses, called involutional melancholia, is quite common, as was observed in Chapter 6. It is marked by insomnia, loss of appetite and weight, irritability, feelings of uselessness and futility ("Life is really over for me."), and fears of death. Like other forms of depression, it responds well to treatment.

HOW TO COPE WITH LOSSES

If the male menopause is primarily a psychological loss experience, the most obvious way to counteract it is to replace the lost gratifications with new ones. Hopefully, a man will begin the replacement process before the losses occur. There are four kinds of gratifications that must be replaced.

1. *Loss of Outlets for Discharge of Aggressive Energy.* Changes in physical abilities, sexual activities, competition for advancement, and diminishing social activities alter the ways in which aggressive energy can be discharged. When such activities are lessened, some avenues for the constructive use of aggressive energy are cut off.

2. *Loss of Sources of Affection and of Persons to Whom to Give Affection.* With the departure of children, sometimes a decrease in sexual activity, a narrowing circle of friends, and loss of particular friends through death, there are fewer ways of obtaining love, support, and esteem. Equally important, there are fewer objects available for feelings of affection.

3. *Loss of Adult Identity.* With the tendency to feel emasculated, with the reawakening of dependency conflicts, and

with the feeling of uselessness, a man's image of himself is somewhat shaken. It is at this point that he often asks if his efforts were worthwhile, and wonders if he has taken the right life path.

4. *Loss of Adventure in Living.* The feeling of having settled into a niche or rut means that one experiences repetitive dullness or boredom. When a man is twenty-one, his world holds promise of romance, excitement, and stimulating new experiences as an adult. In middle age, there is often the feeling that there is nothing new under the sun. While it is perfectly acceptable for the young man to be a dreamer, to call a middle-aged man a dreamer is to criticize him. He is supposed to live in the hard world of facts.

AVENUES OF REPLACEMENT

Replacement for these losses is not necessarily a complex task, but the replacements must fit the personality and preferences of the person. Whether any specific activity will satisfy any given person, only he can tell. We can specify only the general directions in which replacements may be sought.

A superior, in his discussion with such a man, might point out three important ways to replace lost gratifications:

1. Finding new avenues for discharging aggressions constructively in activities he likes
2. Finding new friends
3. Finding new adventure

A wide range of activities can provide these gratifications. Sometimes all three can be obtained in a single activity.

The most important way to renew one's gratifications is through the serious development of a responsible activity that can be carried into retirement. A local manager of a utility company, with considerable information available to him about local economic conditions, began to develop a housing project. A lawyer with an interest in history published his first book on Lincoln in his middle years. The vice-president of one of the major divisions of a steel company has become an authority on Japanese prints. A fifty-five year old dentist, who always wanted to be a merchant, bought a drug store with a small down payment and now devotes a part of his time to each job. A personnel officer bought a small summer place in the woods where he soon built another cabin to rent to hunters and fishermen; his plan is to expand it.

These examples could be multiplied many times over. They have several ingredients in common. They all have the character of work. That is, they require investment of time, energy, and some money. They require continued, consistent effort. They have the opportunity for achievement. They bring the person into necessary contact with other people over with whom they have something important in common. And in each activity, whatever the person does is *his*. Taken together, these ingredients help a man maintain an image of himself as an active, developing man.

Although businesslike activities are the most important source of gratification in our culture, they are not the only activities a man can undertake. Deliberately seeking out other people, learning about them and establishing friendly relationships with those whom one likes, serves both parties alike. For many people it is not easy to find friends; yet loneliness is such a common experience that it has become a major theme for novelists and playwrights. Often, when someone takes the initiative, he finds that the other person wanted very much to establish a social relationship but simply did not know how to begin.

A specific activity in this direction could be public service. There is a desperate need in all areas of public service for people who are willing to lend a hand. Volunteer service on a personal basis in a hospital or some other institutional setting—a boys' club, USO, a rehabilitation center—provides for many a good combination of gratifications. In these organizations, it does not matter where a man is in the social or business hierarchy. He is important to another human being because he can give affection. This kind of psychological transfusion is no less important to some people than a blood transfusion would be to others. And what is more, such an activity requires that a person be at the appointed place at a given time. Nothing demonstrates a man's usefulness more than the demand that he must live up to his promise because another person is depending on him.

Activities with children and adolescents can be especially important. Vitality is a corollary of youth. Zest, curiosity, imagination, and affection can be found among youth in abundance. As a man grows older, he should broaden his base of acquaintances chronologically downward to be able to have the stimulation in youth. In addition, as he grows older, he will have fewer contemporaries, so the more younger friends he has, the less likely he is to become isolated.

Many people make excellent use of pets—particularly those people who are too isolated to make friends.

Feelings of romance and excitement can be renewed in leisurely travel, particularly with friends, seeing new and different sights. A man who learned Spanish in night school took several trips to South America. But he passed up all the churches, night life, and organized tours. He was a simple man with simple interests, so he went from one small town to another, talking to ordinary people as he went. They were as curious about him as he was about them. Since he could speak their language, he was frequently invited to their homes. A by-product of this quite ordinary activity was a new kind of adventure at home: Service clubs wanted to hear how other people really thought and felt. As a result of his lectures, the man developed a new circle of friends in his own community.

One of the most readily available ways of finding new gratifications is in adult education courses. Not enough businessmen take advantage of these courses, although their participation is increasing. These courses cover almost every conceivable subject; in many ways, they are ideal for the middle-aged man. He may select a topic new to him, or refresh his knowledge on familiar subjects. Some companies even pay tuition for such courses if the employee completes them successfully. The other participants are usually people of his own age range. In this activity it will make no difference what his position is or how much money he has. The methods of teaching adult education classes are more likely to fit the immediate needs of the people who participate rather than to be directed toward preconceived formal goals like a degree. As a result, such classes usually are practical and down to earth. In smaller communities, where there may be fewer facilities for adult education, a man may take correspondence courses. If he invites friends to share such courses with him, so much the better.

This is the time in life when a man has an opportunity to do something he always wanted to do—hobbies, a new career, or some novel experience. Almost everyone has some dream to fulfill, some ungratified wish. Free of some of the responsibilities of parenthood, and still a long way from retirement, middle age is the time to do it. And he need not be concerned about justifying to his neighbors what he wants to do. It is his life, not theirs, and his dream.

Many of these activities also involve physical activity—sports, walking, gardening—in which the large, voluntary muscles are used. So much the better for both physical and psychological health.

The man who anticipates some of his possible psychological losses and tries to do something about them actually does himself two good turns. He alleviates much of the pain of middle age, and consequently avoids even more painful experiences later on. The methods he evolves for coping with his change of life are also his preparation for retirement. The superior who can help him do so makes a significant contribution to both man and organization.

RETIREMENT

Nearly a million and a half people reach retirement age each year. Even the population of those seventy-five and over increases by nearly 200,000 each year. The aged population is expected to double before the year 2000. Such a significant population trend has direct import for management because of the obligations management has assumed for long-term relationships with employees.

No matter how successful the adaptation to mid-life problems has been, there are inevitably new adaptations that have to be made in retirement. The most difficult problem for many men is giving up their relationship to the organization. Not many people in executive ranks really want to retire. People for whom the work organization has been a very important part of their lives, are suddenly no longer in the swim. They often feel they are on the discard heap while they still have much to contribute. More painful for some is the loss of power. As long as they were active executives, they were powerful people, both in the organization and in the community. Without a place in the organization, they lose their leverage in the community. For this reason, they are seldom interested in starting volunteer work for the first time after they have retired. It does not mean much to them at that point. To advise retiring executives to devote themselves to fishing or hobbies is inane. Certainly, hobbies can be important avocational interests, and for some they can even become as important as work was. But most men need something in addition, something that provides more self-respect. That usually means some form of business or work.

The company should have some type of preretirement counseling program which recognizes that these men really do not want to retire from an organization to which they have given the better part of a lifetime. Such a program helps to avoid the dread of retirement, preretirement anger toward the company, other psychological symptoms, and the possibility of withdrawal into a futile waiting for death after retirement. A program also makes it possible to counteract resistance to the possibility of retirement, which otherwise leads to an abrupt confrontation with reality at sixty-five. It furthermore reduces the guilt feelings of those who remain and diminishes the feeling of rejection of those who retire.

Both husband and wife can be brought together for retirement planning, if the husband is willing. In one company, when the husbands were invited to bring their wives to such discussions, the wives did not come. Subsequent investigation disclosed that the husbands failed to tell them that they were invited. There are many reasons why men may not want their wives involved. Some may already be concerned about how their wives will view them when they are no longer working. These men may feel a loss of self-esteem if they are counseled in the presence of their wives. Some may want to keep their wives completely dependent upon them, or conversely, to be free of pressure from their wives. The company program should therefore point out that many wives survive their husbands, that therefore wives often have to make financial decisions with limited prior experience, and that a man can undo his best intentions by the simple mistake of not informing his wife.

If husband and wife can be brought together for retirement planning, in most cases this will strengthen the family unit for the transition. Joint planning also serves as another device for counteracting the workings of denial. Here, for example, is how denial may operate in the absence of a formal program:

A company president talked at some length with his immediate vice-president about the company's future and the vice-president's future. The vice-president, then sixty, would retire in five years according to long-accepted policy. The president said that in the company's interest, the vice-president should find and train a successor. He asked also what plans the vice-president had for his retirement. The vice-president said he had none. The president suggested that perhaps the vice-president would want to begin discussing retirement plans with his wife. He added that if the vice-president wanted to talk about such plans with him, he would be glad to do so. He wanted the vice-president to know that he was welcome to make use of the company's staff resources to help make his plans. The vice-president expressed his thanks for the president's interest, saying that he would begin to work on the problem of a successor and to think of his personal plans.

Nearly a year later, when there had been no word about either a successor or personal plans, the president raised the questions again. The vice-president said that he had not been able to find a suitable successor and that while he had thought about retirement plans, he had not yet come to specific conclusions. The president said that they could delay no longer in finding a successor. He and the vice-president talked about the kind of an understudy they wanted to have. They narrowed their alternatives and evolved a plan for screening possible candidates. During the next few months they met regularly to appraise the candidates. By the end of the second year they had selected a man whom they appointed as assistant vice-president. But the vice-president still had no plans for retirement.

Inasmuch as the vice-president's retirement plans were his personal business, the president felt he could not intrude further. From time to time in casual conversation he asked the vice-president about the state of his planning, but these queries drew only noncommittal replies. The years passed. Shortly before the vice-president's sixty-fifth birthday, the two were talking about the vice-president's impending retirement. In startled surprise the vice-president said, "You're not really going to retire me, are you? My wife and I were talking about it just the other day. We both agreed that after all the years I have given to this company, you certainly wouldn't make me retire." His voice rose in anguish as he spoke. He ran from the president's office in tears. He did not return to the company.

A good preretirement counseling program should cover four major areas:

1. *It should provide general retirement advice.* This includes information about social security, pension, health

insurance, benefits for the wife if she survives her husband, and advice on wills and investments. Not all this information and advice has to be given in or by the company, but a company program should make provision for it, and as already emphasized, wives should be informed as well as their husbands, if possible. Much of this information and advice can begin at age sixty and be discussed at intervals until retirement. This makes for gradual adaptation and reasonable planning.

2. *It should provide medical and psychological advice.* Retirement is a radical change, no matter what the preparation. It represents an important psychological loss to most people, about which they have considerable feeling. Sometimes these feelings, particularly anger, are so strong that they interfere with rational planning and adaptation. It is important, therefore, that each person of retirement age have an opportunity to discuss his feelings with a skilled counselor. Having done that, he should talk over the alterations that will occur in his life because of retirement, what contacts, and social experiences he will lose, how his standard of living will change his health status, and what plans he has for coping with these changes. But the counselor should not be a young and inexperienced personnel clerk. Companies would be wise to seek out retired psychiatric social workers for such counseling positions. If there is not enough retirement business in a company to make such a counseling program feasible, then a number of companies might sponsor a counselor in the local guidance clinic or family service agency.

3. *It should provide business advice.* A good many executives would prefer to go from their companies to some small business of their own. Some have done so. Although many small businesses are losing out in competition with larger

units, there are still opportunities for new businesses, particularly those that offer specialized products or services. Large businesses must concentrate on those products and services that generate volume. This leaves opportunities for the man who will be both selective in his choice and modest in his ambitions. A man, with the experience of a working lifetime, might be able to offer that experience as a consultant to others who might not have been able to hire him at his previous salary. Someone who always wanted to undertake a business venture, but could not because his family needed income, might now do so. With a pension or other income, a retired man is freer to undertake limited ventures on which he does not have to count for income.

It would be helpful to those who are interested in a small business to have information on what kinds of opportunities exist. Research departments of schools of business usually have much local information. More general guidance is available from the Small Business Administration, state industrial development commissions, the U.S. Department of Commerce. Sometimes local bankers know of businesses that might be purchased, as do real estate brokers who specialize in businesses. Information about business opportunities in warmer climates might even be obtained from Chambers of Commerce. There are many sources from which such information could be compiled for the study of prospective retirees.

Some may question the need for such a service for those who have been businessmen all their lives. It is an interesting phenomenon, however, that executives, despite their experience, have difficulty seeking out and "selling" themselves into new positions when they have lost their jobs. Executive recruiters flourish for this among other reasons. In a sense, the executive who seeks a new business connection is like a physician who becomes ill or a lawyer who is being sued. Each needs professional counsel by someone who is not emotionally involved in his problem. And the executive who can retire to another business is likely to find challenge and gratification in his retirement. In short, he can make good use of a specialized kind of vocational guidance.

4. *It should provide advice on relocation.* Information about housing, services, cost of living, temperature, population, and so on is readily available for every community in the country. Much of it could be assembled for the inspection and consideration of the prospective retiree, if he wants to move to another community.

Some companies have a gradual retirement policy: a month's vacation at sixty, two months at sixty-one, and formal retirement at sixty-five. This gradual increase in vacation time can be very useful, provided it is not used merely as more time to sit around. During such periods, the man who is soon to retire can take a look at communities about which he has read, or can look more closely into business opportunities suggested by his study and his discussion with the retirement counselor.

A good source of information about retirement planning programs is *Retirement Planning,* Personnel Methods Series No. 12, U.S. Civil Service Commission, 1961. This is available from the U.S. Government Printing Office for 20 cents.

Like all other psychological problems, those of aging essentially have to do with maintaining an equilibrium among the many forces at play at any given time. One of the forces is a man's interaction with the organization that employs him. That force can be a tower of strength to him—or indicate that he has wasted his occupational life.

PART IV

THE PROBLEM IN HAND

THIS BOOK HAS DESCRIBED SOME IMPORTANT ASPECTS OF THE WAY the personality works, some symptoms appearing when its balance is disturbed, and some of the situations that disturb its balance. But what can you do when someone is emotionally upset and it is your responsibility to do something about it? What general principles should guide you? What are your limits? When do you turn to a professional for help?

These considerations, which should be obvious by this time, are basic:

All behavior is motivated, much of it by thoughts and feelings of which the person himself is not aware. Behavior does not occur by chance. As has been noted in this book, ego, id, superego, and environment are all sources of motivation. Every thought and every act occurs as a resultant of these forces. Behavior is subject to scientific laws. To a certain extent, it is predictable. It is therefore possible for the study of behavior to be a science and for behavior to be changed by various techniques such as education and psychotherapy. Often, when behavior appears to occur by chance, when it is surprising, that means that not enough is known about the forces which caused it. Often, people do not want to believe that their own behavior did not occur accidentally, for they do not want to face the hostile part of their personalities. Nor do they want to believe that another man's behavior might have been due to forces beyond his awareness and control. For then they would have to give up many long-cherished beliefs about the effects of punishment and the sadistic gratification so many people get when, as in the case of a criminal, a man is punished severely. If behavior occurred by chance, no one could understand it.

Everyone has the continuing task of maintaining his psychological equilibrium. At any give time, any one of us may be listing slightly to starboard or trying to keep from being buffeted by a sudden emotional storm. Despite these pressures, a person must nevertheless continue living, correcting for list as best he can, or conserving strength to ride out the storm. Each will defend himself the best way he knows how. As he does so, the more energy he must devote to defense, the less he will have for forward movement.

At some point in life, almost everyone will be emotionally disturbed or upset. For a few hours, a few days, a few weeks, a man may be irritable or angry ("I got up on the wrong side of the bed"), or blue ("I'm feeling low today"), or hypersensitive. When he feels like this, when he has difficulty maintaining an equilibrium, he is emotionally disturbed. He cannot work as well as he usually does. It is more difficult for him to keep up his relationships with other people. He may feel hopeless or helpless.

But just because he is mildly emotionally disturbed does not mean he needs professional help or hospitalization. A cold is a minor form of upper respiratory infection, the extreme of which is pneumonia. If you have a cold, that does not mean you will have pneumonia. Even if you do get pneumonia, with present treatment methods most people recover, and the same is true of mental illness. The difference between the mild and severe is one of degree, not of kind. It is just more of the same thing.

Furthermore, as has been indicated, other people are affected by how a person feels and behaves, as he is affected by their feelings and behavior. Disequilibrium, mental illness, is there-

fore to some degree *communicable*. The problems of the parents have their effects on the children, those of the executive on his subordinates, and vice versa. The problems precipitated in the office or plant are carried home to the family, and the same is true in reverse. Often the subtle feelings transmitted from one person to another cannot be traced. Yet the feelings are just as real and just as potent as bacteria.

Because no one has had either perfect heredity or perfect environment, everyone has his weak spots. When the balance of forces is such that there is stress where he is weak, he will have difficulty. The incidence of mental illness, then, is not one out of twenty or some other proportionate statistic. Rather it is one out of one!

CHAPTER 15

Emotional First Aid

AT ANY ONE TIME, EACH PERSON IS DOING THE BEST HE CAN, as a result of the multiple forces that bring about any given behavior. A change in the forces is required to bring about a change in behavior. The most significant force, as has been mentioned, is that which supports the ego and strengthens the person—love in its broadest sense.

Love neutralizes aggression and diminishes hostility. "A soft word turneth away wrath," says the old aphorism. Genuine demonstration of love in the broad sense is the keystone to the diminution of hostile feelings and the success of emotional first aid. It is the strongest and most effective support of the ego. To give love in this sense does not mean maudlin expressions, but rather actions that reflect esteem and regard for the other person as a human being.

There is another reason why the action of a human being is important emotional first aid. Emotional disturbances always involve impairment of relationship with others. When a man is angry or sad, he cannot be cordial. If he becomes highly excited, it is difficult for others to understand him or to keep pace with him. If he develops "nervous headaches" or some other physical symptom, and takes to his bed, he is out of touch with others for at least a short time.

Since emotional disturbance is so often a product of impaired relations with others, people frequently gain the psychological strength to cope more effectively with their problems by experiencing more constructive relationships. Therefore, your own personality and the way you relate yourself to others are the most important helping devices available.

Your first concern when you see the need for help is to doubt whether you have any right to intrude. This concern is invariably voiced by business executives.

WHEN DO YOU HELP?

There are only two circumstances in which you are permitted to intrude into another person's privacy.

He may ask you for help, as a friend and associate. By doing so, he makes his problem your business.

His job performance, for which you are responsible, may be impaired. He should know about it. Sometimes, when you recognize that a person is upset, you are reluctant to add to his burdens by telling him that he is falling down on the job. But no business can permit job performance to deteriorate. Often, calling a man's attention to his work performance may enable him to talk about his problem or to seek professional help. Thus you should state the job situation factually and clearly.

By way of illustration, a thirty-four-year-old plant manager, though new to the organization, was making a satisfactory profit. He had earned the support of his local group and satisfactorily handled rapid expansion and assimilation of new product lines. Despite his apparent success, members of the headquarters staff felt that he was incompetent.

When they visited him, he did not seem to know his job, did not seem to provide leadership, was impolitic and sometimes rude. He appeared to have a completely blank expression and asked questions whose answers he already knew. He seldom allowed his visitors to know what he was thinking or even that he could think.

When these complaints came to the division manager, he took them seriously enough to go to the plant and spend a week there. During the course of the week, the plant manager talked freely to the manager. The plant manager complained about the headquarters group in some detail, working off his resentment of it. As the two men continued to talk, toward the end of the week, the plant manager began to discuss his own family history and to speak of how and why he tended to withdraw into himself when he thought he was likely to be criticized. He also said that he often asked many questions of others to keep them from asking questions of him. These were the two aspects of his behavior that led people to think of him as cold and stupid; so, when he mentioned them, the division manager reported the complaints he had received and their relationship to the behavior which the man himself described. Since the man was already aware of his own behavior pattern and the criticisms were directly related to what he had already said of himself, he was able to take the division manager's comments.

The division manager then talked further about the importance of lowering his barriers to communicate with people. Apparently, as a result of the interest and support of the division manager, the plant manager was able to improve his behavior sufficiently, and there were no further complaints from the headquarters staff.

HOW DO YOU KNOW THAT A PERSON NEEDS HELP?

Emotional disturbance is seen in the manifestations of prolonged or excessive anxiety. To summarize, there are three major signs of emotional distress when a person's ordinary means of warding off excessive or prolonged anxiety are not adequate. All involve change of behavior.

1. The person's usual manner may be overemphasized. A quiet person may become even more withdrawn. A well-ordered person may become overconcerned with details. The hail-fellow-well-met salesman may increase his pace until he is described as "jet-propelled." These people are racing their motors, trying to cope with stresses.

2. When increased use of the customary personality devices does not work effectively, more obvious signs of distress begin to appear. A person may be restless or agitated. He may be unable to concentrate. He may become tense and jittery, perspire freely, feel panicky, and have other symptoms, which were described in Part II as acute and chronic reactions. These symptoms will be evident even to the nonprofessional eye.

3. Radical change in behavior indicates extremely severe stress. The orderly, controlled person may become alcoholic. The quiet person may become noisy and aggressive. Thoughts and ideas that are irrational may appear.

WHAT DO YOU DO WHEN YOU ARE
AWARE OF A PROBLEM?

There are three principles to the helping process:

1. *Act as a friend.* When acting as a friend, you permit the distressed person to feel that it is all right to talk about his problem, that you will help. This provides some immediate relief because the distressed person now knows he can draw on your strength. At the same time, by bringing his problem into the open, he gets additional relief. With the temporary relief these two circumstances give, he can now think more clearly about appropriate further steps.

2. *Listen.* Listening is the most overused word in human relations. Everyone talks about it; few know what it really means. It is the essential step in helping, for to listen is to give understanding. Listening is difficult, but it can have tremendous value.

When you listen to another person, you imply you are willing to help him. To him this means that you believe he is a worthy human being and that you respect him as such.

Listening means that you recognize that the distressed person has to feel as he does. You know that behavior does not occur by chance. He is reacting to forces beyond his awareness. He cannot "snap out of it"; otherwise he would. There is no point in telling him to do so. He does not want to feel the way he does. If he could feel differently he would. But a person cannot stop feeling blue or jittery any more than he can stop having a fever or a headache. When you tell another person, "You don't need to feel that way," you merely indicate your own lack of understanding.

Let the distressed person tell his own story in his own way. Sometimes a point may not be clear, and a question may help clarify it. Other than that, every intrusion disrupts the listening process.

If you indicate you do not understand, by offering clichés or by doing the talking yourself, you are telling the distressed person he has turned to the wrong man for help.

When a person turns to us in distress, we often get a little upset. Sometimes we really wish he would go to someone else. As a result, we may become subtly angry. We may blame him, or tell him what he should have done, or criticize or offer pity, or provide logical answers to questions he has never really asked. To do so is to fail to listen.

In these days of increasing discussion of psychology and human relations, many words are bandied about and there are glib answers for all kinds of questions. Most of them are inappropriate psychologizing of the worst kind. Leave the diagnoses to the professionals.

Each person has his own problems. Those of the next man may strike you as trivial. Your reaction is to become impatient and restless, even if you say nothing. "He thinks he has problems," you say to yourself. When the other person senses this attitude, as he surely will, he will know you are not listening. Though his problems may seem small to you, they are no small matter to him.

It is not easy for a person to take his distress to someone else. To make light of his discomfort is to treat him with disrespect.

Listening is sometimes difficult when the troubled person cannot state his problem clearly. Remember that even under the best of circumstances, it is not easy to express one's feelings. When a person is deeply troubled, it is just that much harder. Sometimes he talks in circles.

Sometimes he cannot talk at all and sits silently. There is a tendency to rush in to say something. When you do, you stop listening.

If a man becomes uncomfortable when listening, he un-wittingly tries to escape. Sometimes he does this by offering a bit of "wisdom." Advice costs nothing. It is one quick way of getting rid of the other person without really having to give him any attention.

Another way of escaping is to make decisions for the person. But this is ineffective. Unless he is too upset to make rational decisions, he must come to his own. The listener's job is to help by being a sounding board against which alternative solutions may be tried. Making his decisions for him only creates resentment.

There is one exception. If the distressed person cannot control himself, someone else will have to assume control. Few of even the most disturbed people are dangerous or violent. They are terribly frightened. They do not know what is happening to them. A familiar face, a comforting friend, will provide a stable reference point and some relief from fear.

3. *Limit.* You are an executive, not a psychotherapist, or counselor. These two facts draw your limits of action.

You cannot go beyond the ordinary means of supervision available in your company. If you cannot solve a problem within the channels you have, then it is time to refer the person to a professional.

When you have not been able to help the person solve his problem in an interview or two, rarely more, it is time to send him for help. This assumes, of course, that you have been communicating with your subordinates regularly and that these interviews are not substitutes for ordinary and necessary supervisory sessions.

You will not be able to solve all problems which come to you, nor even a significant proportion of them. Too many executives carry a sense of guilt because they have not solved human relations problems, many of which would defy a skilled psychologist or psychiatrist. Here is a case in point:

The assistant to the president had been with the company thirty-five years and was within two years of retirement. When the president talked with him about his projected retirement, he disagreed with the compulsory retirement policy. He tried to bring pressure on the president through friends not to retire him.

A year before the retirement date, the president again talked to him. It was apparent the assistant had made no plans. He had not talked even to his wife about retirement.

Six months before retirement he had a heart attack, so he was not able to continue working as he had before. Despite this new problem, he would not even talk about his forthcoming retirement.

Shortly before the date of his retirement, he came to the president with tears in his eyes, presenting many problems he thought would occur when he retired. He was given a two-month extension, by which time he thought he would have solved some of the problems and be ready to retire. When the two months were up, he asked for another extension. It was denied.

Here, despite repeated efforts by the president to counsel with the man and to help him deal with approaching retirement, he could not accept the fact. The president handled the situation reasonably. Perhaps he could have been more direct and firm. But the realities he stated were denied by his assistant. Such a denial of reality presented a problem beyond the capacity of a layman. It would not have been easy even for a professional to help him face and deal with reality.

You will not be of much help to the person with long-standing chronic and repetitive problems. Nor will you be able to help the person who is already showing signs of severe distress—panic, agitation, marked behavior changes, suicidal threats. He needs to be in professional hands. And do not minimize suicidal threats. Let the professional decide whether he means it.

You will be able to help the person whose stress results from some acute job or family difficulty.

WHY DOES LISTENING HAVE SUCH POWERFUL EFFECTS?

When a person talks about his problems, he releases the feelings that have been held in. This release eases their pressure. If he has feelings of fear or guilt that are not clear to him, he clarifies and dissipates them by talking about them. He not only finds a friend in the listener, but also he has that rare experience of understanding and acceptance from someone whom he regards as an authority figure. Practically no one has an opportunity to have someone else listen to him freely in this world under nonemergency circumstances. Yet everyone wants to be heard. Finally, a man often gets some insight into the way his feelings affect his behavior and why others may react to him as they do. Therefore listening is interpreted by the person who is upset as an act of faith. It helps to restore the person's confidence in other people and thereby makes it easier for him to deal with them. It also restores some of his self-confidence and alleviates some of his fears of what might happen to him. These, taken together, add immeasurably to the ego strength of a person.

WHEN SHOULD YOU EXERCISE
PARTICULAR CARE?

When a person in distress turns to another for help, he does so as an act of trust. He reveals himself, believing the other person will help. He may feel free to express his anger or his fears, even to the point of tears, because he feels his confidence will not be violated.

The listener may be embarrassed or even angered by a demonstration of emotion. He should recognize such behavior as an act of trust and not be dismayed. Above all, he must not violate his own integrity by talking about what has been confided to him.

When a person is distressed, it may be difficult for him to remember what has been discussed and what conclusions were reached. Often it helps to summarize the results before he leaves, particularly if he is to take additional steps toward help.

Sometimes a person may later feel he said too much. This feeling can be so strong that he may ignore the person whose help he sought. Such behavior should be anticipated. It may be avoided if, before the distressed person leaves the office, the listener indicates that feelings of dismay or regret for having confided are not unnatural or unusual.

WHAT ABOUT REFERRAL?

People who should be referred to professional sources of help include those who act irrationally, such as those who hear voices, talk to themselves consistently, or believe that imaginary things are happening to them. People who speak of suicide or make suicidal attempts, those who threaten others with physical violence, those who commit repeated offenses against the law or the rules of the organization, those who are paralyzed by their inability to make decisions, those who have constant physical symptoms or disturbing mannerisms that they cannot control—all should be referred. Occasionally people seeking help are your friends or have a relationship with you that is either too close for you to be objective or for them to be comfortable confiding in you. Such people should be referred.

Referral can be extremely helpful to people who have considerable promise but who seem to stand in their own way. These are the up-and-coming young "Yes, but . . ." men. Everyone agrees that they demonstrate ability, but one or another aspect of their personality makes their superiors hesitate about advancing them. Often such men can prosper after they have had professional help. This case is an example:

> Martin Fowler was put in charge of expanding his firm's newest division, which had not been going well. He did an excellent job of bringing his part of the business from near chaos to smooth functioning. He soon earned the respect of his own colleagues as well as that of the company's leading customers.
>
> Fowler was thirty-six. Because he had a severely handicapped daughter, he developed few interests outside his work and spent much of his time helping his wife take care of this child and their other two children. Knowing of his problem, his colleagues did not criticize him for his limited social activities. They knew that on the job he was thorough, and because of his knowledge he had saved considerable amounts of money for his company's customers. His major fault was that he did not get things done quickly.

After Fowler had been with the company three years, he began to be absent frequently because of illness. It was about this time that his superior left the company. Fowler was not placed under his superior's successor, but was given coordinate status, which required close cooperation with him. The two could not seem to communicate or coordinate. They criticized and blamed each other. To resolve this situation, an important part of Fowler's work was assigned to someone else so that these two would not have to be in contact with each other. Fowler did not like this administrative action.

While the disagreement between Fowler and his colleague was at its height, Fowler's secretary asked for another assignment. She told the personnel director she could not work for a man who would not stand up for himself and retreated into illness. Fowler also began to have problems with others in the company, primarily because he was failing to be forthright enough to work with them. Thus he began to close off more and more opportunities to grow in the over-all company structure. To these problems were added the growing complaints from customers and colleagues.

A vice-president who had known Fowler since he started in the company talked at length with him about his problem. Knowing that Fowler was under medical care, he asked Fowler's permission to talk with his doctor. Fowler seemed pleased that someone was interested in him and granted permission. In his discussion with the doctor, the vice-president told him of Fowler's work problems and sought the doctor's advice. The doctor reported that he had suggested to Fowler that he seek psychiatric advice, but Fowler was procrastinating just as he procrastinated in his work. The doctor suggested that the vice-president tell Fowler he would lose his job unless he did something about his problem.

When the vice-president took this firm position, Fowler sought professional help. He began to show considerable improvement. He placed his handicapped daughter in an institution, which relieved both him and his wife of a heavy burden at home. He seemed happy to work under a new department head and showed enough progress that he was soon assuming some of his old responsibilities and reaching out for new ones. At the time the case was written, he had already had two promotions.

TO WHOM DO YOU REFER?

Every person in a position of responsibility should have someone to turn to for guidance when emotional emergencies arise. If there is a company medical department, that should be his first source of help. Outside the business there are psychiatrists, clinical psychologists, and psychiatric social workers. In many cases, help is available at the other end of the telephone, particularly in larger communities where there are family service agencies, mental hygiene clinics, out-patient clinics, and alcoholism clinics. The family physician of the troubled person is often a good source of help and guidance.

On some occasion you may want to know how to judge the competence of a given professional person. This is not easy for the layman, or even the physician, to do. The best yardsticks available to you are professional training and approval, which can be checked in professional directories.

A qualified psychiatrist is a licensed physician who has completed his medical training, an internship, and three additional years of psychiatric residency or training in a hospital approved for such training by the American Medical Association. After a physician has completed this training and has had two more years of experience, he is then eligible for examination by the American Board of Psychiatry and Neurology. If he passes this examination, he is certified as a diplomate of the Board, and thereafter is often referred to as "Board-certified." Such a person is formally qualified in the eyes of his professional colleagues as a specialist in psychiatry. Some psychiatrists, in addition, take advanced training in psychoanalysis. The director of the American Psychiatric Association lists all psychiatrists who are members of that association and indicates which are certified. The directory of the American Medical Association lists the training and qualifications of all members of that association.

A qualified clinical psychologist is one who has completed his Ph.D. in psychology from a recognized university and has taken an internship of one or more years in a hospital or clinic. The American Psychological Association approves certain university programs and clinical training centers, which are listed annually in *The American Psychologist*. After completing this training and a total of five years of experience, two of which must be in a supervised clinical setting, the clinical psychologist is then eligible for certification by the American Board of Examiners in Professional Psychology (ABEPP). If he passes this examination, he is recognized as a diplomate of the Board and is regarded by his colleagues as qualified for independent professional practice. In many, but not all, states he will also be licensed or certified by a state board if he offers private services. Some clinical psychologists will take post-doctoral clinical training in hospitals or clinics, and a few will take advanced training in psychoanalysis. The directory of the American

Psychological Association lists all psychologists who are members of that association and indicates which are certified and by whom.

A qualified social worker has a master's degree in social work from a university graduate program in social work approved by the Council on Social Work Education. This includes two 9-months' field experiences, carried on concurrently with academic training, in two different agencies, approved by the university graduate program. Membership in the National Association of Social Workers requires a master's degree. After two consecutive years of experience in a social work agency after getting a master's degree, a social worker is eligible for certification by the Academy of Certified Social Workers (ACSW). If he is certified, the initials ACSW appear after his name on his certificate, which means that he has attained the highest formal level in his profession. Some, in addition, take a year of post-master's work in approved clinics, agencies, or hospitals. Qualified social workers are listed in the directory of the National Association of Social Workers. Very few are in private practice, however. Most are found in family service agencies, guidance or mental hygiene clinics, and mental hospitals.

If you want to find a directory or the name of a professional person from a directory, all university departments of psychiatry, psychology, and social work have directories of their professions. County medical societies have medical directories. Local mental health associations frequently publish lists of mental health resources and will provide information about resources by phone. Information about professional preparation and qualifications is so readily available that no person need consult another person in ignorance of his qualifications. However, you should recognize that official credentials are only minimum educational and experiential qualifications. They cannot be guaranties of quality of service. In some measure, quality depends on individual skill. But it also depends on the rapport between the person seeking help and the professional to whom he turns. And rapport is a very personal matter.

If the person must be referred for professional help, it is best done in a matter-of-fact way. It is important to help the person understand that something is wrong for which he can get help, using physical illness as an analogy. It is certainly appropriate to suggest that the problem calls for help from someone who is professionally trained to deal with such problems. The suggestion of referral is essentially the opening of another avenue of help.

If, however, the person feels he is being passed off or that he is viewed as crazy, hopeless, or just not worth attention, he will not take advantage of the referral. The attitude of of the listener in suggesting referral is probably as important as any other single factor in whether additional help is sought. Unless you are convinced that referral will help him, he is unlikely to follow through or, if he does follow through, to stick with it.

In making a referral, you should be guided by this fundamental consideration. Once you recognize illness or disequilibrium that interferes with the job, you have a right to expect that the person who suffers will do the responsible thing for his illness. The principle is no different for emotional illness than for a physical illness. There is no reason to blame the person for his illness, but he should recognize his responsibility to make use of the help available to him. When, as in Fowler's case, you take a firm stand about the need for help, you are not being unsympathetic about his problem. You are, and rightfully, unsympathetic about his failure to use available resources to do something about it. Furthermore, as a responsible executive, you cannot permit his performance to deteriorate or the organization to suffer without taking some action to prevent both.

Even when the referral has been made, it is important for the person to know that the listener is standing by to help further if he can. A source of psychological support is an important need in everyone's life.

And what about your own mental health? Some of the ideas in this book may be helpful to you. Beyond that, keep a watchful eye on yourself. If you find that you are having continuing difficulties which interfere with your work or with gratifying relationships with other people, then you, too, should be wise enough to seek professional help.

PART V

WHAT NEXT?

———————

We have seen some aspects of the interrelationship of organizational activities and the psychology of the individual, and the manner in which you and the organization can support the individual in his efforts to maintain his equilibrium. Your major concern goes beyond problems of individuals as such to maintaining organizational regeneration and survival. What can psychoanalytic theory contribute to the task? What are the implications of this discussion for avoiding conflict among individuals, developing executive talent, and making more rational decisions?

The more clearly you can understand and act on the basis of reality and psychological fact, the more effectively you enable people to maintain their mental health and help the organization to survive and grow. After examining problems of executive development, this discussion will turn to an examination of personality clashes. It will then be possible to review many different management practices, to see how they may be motivated by guilt feelings rather than more rational considerations.

CHAPTER 16

Executive Development

ALMOST EVERY COMPANY TODAY IS CONCERNED ABOUT THE development of executive talent, to ensure the company's long-run survival. Many companies have undertaken management development programs to meet this need. Although these programs are often of high caliber—carefully planned and well organized—there can be psychological barriers within the organization that subtly counteract the development process.[18]

RELEVANT AXIOMS

To understand the leading obstacles to development, it is important to abstract some of the psychological principles from Part I and Chapter 11 and then examine some contemporary management development practices in light of these principles.

Early influences shape personality. As has been shown, the early relationships of the child in the family play a critical role in character formation, in the evolution of personality traits, and in the development of attitudes toward others.

These early influences are primarily emotional influences.
They have to do with the ways in which people come to
balance and to express the twin forces of love and hate.
Every human being tends to repeat unconsciously those
modes of seeking and giving love and those patterns of expressing his aggressive impulses which he learned in the
family. Thus, people often are reacting emotionally when
they think they are responding intellectually.

*As a result of these early influences, organizations tend to
assume qualities much like those of the family.* This is tacitly
recognized in business circles in the phrase, "We're just like
one big family," and in the many efforts of business organizations to facilitate the identification of the employee with the
organization. In the work situation, a person unconsciously
continues to seek many of the gratifications he once obtained
in the family, and to resolve some of the psychological problems that were not resolved at home during the course of
his growth. For example, the pursuit of status and status
symbols may be viewed as an effort to obtain indications of
esteem from authority figures. Psychologically, this pursuit is
little different from the effort of the child to obtain love from
his parents and to vanquish his sibling rivals.

*One of the essential avenues for psychological growth is
the process of identification.* The superego is acquired by
identification with the parents. Identification is also an important medium for establishing one's sex role. A boy has
difficulty learning to become a man unless he can identify
himself with his father and, later, with other parental figures
—teachers, Scout leaders, grandfathers, and so on. All these
figures are men who have more power than he. Given affection and encouragement by such men, and particularly the
freedom to express his own feelings of affection and anger
toward them, he incorporates some of their behavior and

values into his own personality. He acquires some of their power, some greater ability to master both his own impulses and his environment.

In such relationships there is usually rivalry as well. The boy often not only tries to emulate his models, but also to do better than they. Unconsciously he seeks to displace them, to become more powerful than they are. It is out of this rivalry that the spirit of competition is born.

Implicit in these relationships is the boy's dependence on the adult for guidance, direction, and support. Gradually, his independence increases, provided the adult encourages it.

Often a poor or unhappy relationship with the father results in unconscious hate of all authority. Hostility, antagonism, negativism in relation to authority are among the behavioral consequences.

These effects—the acquisition of adult perspectives and powers, the spirit of competition, and growing independence—are products of a relationship. If the relationship is impaired, to a certain extent psychological growth is impaired. A boy may not have a good male model available for identification; his father may be too weak a person with whom to identify, or too harsh and rejecting, or a highly transient figure—or he may have died. In such circumstances, without adequate father substitutes, it becomes difficult for the boy to establish the foundations for evolving his own identity as a unique, independent, mature, adult male.

Identification continues to be a mechanism for growth over a lifetime. No man is so perfect or so self-satisfied that he gives up seeking to attain some of the qualities of other men. All religions hold forth models. During professional training, a man identifies with those more learned in the field. Where it is possible in business or other organizations, he identifies himself with his superiors and thus acquires some of the perspectives, values, attitudes, and behavior required for survival and progress in the organization.

A person carries with him images of identification models, some quite consciously, and strives to meet the expectations these people have (or are thought to have) of him. When executives are asked to discuss their work history, they are likely to mention some older person in business or private life who took a special interest in them. Frequently they will use the phrase, "He was like a father to me." In my experience, rarely is such a person spontaneously mentioned among hourly people and foremen. Although the thesis has not been verified by formal research, it appears that *one of the significant differences between those who become executives and those who do not lies in the presence or absence of certain kinds of identification models.* Some awareness of this phenomenon lies behind the question that is sometimes asked of aspirants to management positions: "Who were your childhood heroes?"

This is not to say that identification alone leads one to become a good executive. Many skills and talents are required. Having a model, then, would seem to be necessary though not sufficient to the development of an executive.

MISSING INGREDIENT

A major factor in psychological growth is the opportunity for a person to identify with those who have more experience, skill, and power than he has. This means that the younger, less experienced men must have continuing personal contact with their superiors in relationships whose quality of encouragement and affection (in the very broad sense of the word) facilitates identification.

No matter how good the formal development program, it cannot replace the personal relationships that are also required for growth. *But the training responsibility is usually assigned to staff people in the organization who, regardless of their competence in their jobs, have very limited authority and power.* Therefore they cannot themselves be adequate identification figures for men who are pursuing increasing line responsibilities. When important operating executives do not play a significant role in management development, it should not be surprising if the man who is being "developed" comes to feel that the process is only an intellectual exercise.

BARRIERS TO COACHING

To cope with this problem, top management frequently supplements the formal training programs with coaching or appraisal systems.[19] In these structured relationships, superiors are to help their subordinates grow into more mature and experienced executives. Superior and subordinate are expected to meet at given intervals, to evaluate the subordinate's experiences, to set future goals, and usually to prepare a written summary of their discussion.

But the coaching and appraisal process, despite its many real and possible values, has not achieved widespread, enthusiastic acceptance. Apparently, it has not yet become the medium for identification that it might be. Why not? Five reasons stand out:

1. *Lack of Time.* Though chronological time may be set aside for coaching and appraisal, the relationship is often limited by time. Even more important is that the superior may not have the "psychological time" to give to the subordinate. That is, he may invest himself only superficially in the coaching process.

Why do superiors lack time? Has not the corporate president agreed that the development of executives is important? Has not the company demonstrated its conviction by spending large amounts of money on the development program?

The answer in both cases is, "Yes, but. . . ." Though the president may have agreed that executive development is important, though a budget may have been provided for the development program, and though provisions may have been made for executives to coach their subordinates, *rarely is an operating executive in a business organization rewarded for developing young executives.* When the president talks with his immediate subordinates, too often his discussion centers around cutting costs, increasing profit margins, developing markets, and so on. Too often he evaluates their performance in these terms. There is nothing wrong with an evaluation that deals with the realities of business life. But when the president, in keeping with certain value orientations described in Chapter 11, appears to be relatively unconcerned, except as an afterthought, about developing his own subordinates, his behavior shows that anyone wanting to help develop others undertakes an extracurricular activity of dubious commercial value.

2. *No Mistakes Allowed.* A vice-president of an electronics firm who had "grown up with the business," reflecting on his experiences, observed that he had made many mistakes in the course of his career and that he had learned much from them. He then added, somewhat to his own surprise, that young executives in his company were no longer so free to make mistakes. Here is a not unusual example:

The branch manager of a far-flung firm traveled considerably. Whenever he was gone from his branch office, his assistant voluntarily, and with his enthusiastic approval, submitted certain information to the main office.

Both the manager and his assistant felt the information was timely and should have been communicated to the main office immediately. The manager either cleared or was informed of all communications. In one of these communications it was apparent that the assistant branch manager misunderstood a company policy. The general manager asked the branch manager to correct his assistant's misunderstanding in a gentle way by clarifying company policy. The branch manager, however, severely reprimanded his assistant, after which the assistant manager's communications ceased, a fact regarded by the general manager as a loss to the company.

The contemporary climate in American business and industry seems to be one in which mistakes are increasingly less tolerated or permitted. With ever larger amounts of money at stake, with increasing amounts of data on which to base decisions, and with continuing expansion of rules, policies, and procedures, there is a concomitant demand for levels of performance that more closely approach perfection. This demand is intellectually stimulating, but it forces executives into many conflict situations.

For example, the general results obtained are never good enough in many companies, leading to more pressure from superiors for improvement rather than help toward growth. This pressure is often viewed as punishment for mistakes, and as a result, the subordinate learns not to make mistakes by not demonstrating initiative. In turn, the superior is required to tell the subordinate what to do, which prevents learning.[20]

Often the subordinates amass reams of data on all kinds of obscure questions just in case someone should ask for some isolated bit of information. Endless hours of countless staff people are devoted to compiling reports whose sole purpose is to prove that the executive is "on top of" his job. However, the "just in case" files are never really enough to allay the kind of insecurity that brings them about. All too many executives feel that they must know their subordinates' work in detail, just in case they are asked about it. As a result, they constantly intrude on the work of their subordinates.

The punishment for mistakes, leading to less initiative and greater direction, makes subordinates feel stupid. The repetitive futility of the "just in case" files angers them. They feel they are not trusted. These feelings alienate the subordinates from the superior, making identification difficult. In addition, the close supervision leaves little time to cultivate personal (but task-centered) relationships with subordinates. Such behavior vitiates the effects of even the ideal formal development program.

3. *Dependency Needs Rejected.* In Chapter 1, it was explained that each person has the psychological task of weaning himself from his dependent relationship with his parents in order to become a mature adult. No matter how successfully a person may resolve this problem, everyone continues to have unconscious wishes to be dependent. Some people can accept these wishes and lean on other people in acceptable ways and at appropriate times; as, for example, when they are ill and need care. Others must reject their own dependency wishes and go to great lengths to demonstrate that they do not need to lean on anyone else at any time for anything.

Any person who is responsible for the work performance of subordinates is required to let other people lean on him in the sense that, to varying degrees, they must turn to him for decisions, direction, and encouragement. This is not an easy psychological position for a superior because most people have enough trouble dealing with their own dependency wishes without having to accept the dependence of subordinates.

As a result, many executives have difficulty with increasing responsibility for other people. Such responsibility can be more easily handled if they in turn have adequate support from their own superiors. But how often do they get it? Failing to recognize the difference between legitimate needs and overdependence, a typically hard-boiled executive may well reject the subordinates' needs, saying, "Let them stand on their own two feet. I've always had to stand on my own feet. I'm not going to baby them. If they fail, I'll lower the boom." Such a remark is usually made in anger, an indication of the executive's problem with his own unconscious wishes to be dependent.

When the superior sees only those two alternatives of rejection ("stand on your own feet") or direct interference ("lower the boom"), he has no sense of how to help without fostering dependence. His black-or-white extremes exclude a middle ground—that of seeking out reasons for difficulties and helping subordinates with them.

When the senior executive fails to meet the legitimate dependency needs of his own subordinates, he (1) increases the stresses for the subordinate and (2) makes it more difficult for the man in turn to accept the dependency of his subordinates. Identification does not flower under these circumstances.

In addition, the senior executive himself is necessarily dependent on the subordinate to get the work done. The executive who cannot accept his own dependency needs is likely to be angry with himself and his assistant because he must be dependent on the latter. Such strong feelings of hostility are usually repressed, but they appear indirectly in the superior's attempt to make the subordinate an extension of himself. For example:

> One capable but authoritarian engineering executive invariably responds to his subordinate's request for help on a problem with quick solutions "off the top of his head." However, what the subordinate wants is psychological support from the superior in the form of discussion of the problem and exploration of alternatives. The superior does not know how to give such support—the superior wants the subordinate to implement the "quick solutions," and this is impossible because the "solutions" have been offered before enough questions have been asked. As a result, they do not fit the complexity of the problems.
>
> The superior wants the subordinate to be an extension of himself, to respond as he has responded. "What did you do about what I said?" he asks. Yet the subordinate, also a mature adult, cannot be simply an extension of the superior. He can, however, be one who helps and assists the superior, provided the latter can accept him in that role. When the senior man cannot accept his dependence, the subordinate cannot feel that he has support, that he is recognized as an individual. The superior's hostility is reflected in his inability to "let go" of the subordinate. The subordinate responds with chronic hostility of his own. Their relationship is an uneasy one.

A superior like this one is also likely to feel that his subordinate is not good enough to represent him. The subordinate never can, in fact, seem good enough in such situations, for the superior's underlying insecurity will not permit him to think anyone good enough. The subordinate is inevitably victimized.

4. *Rivalry Repressed*. Although he may not be conscious of such feelings or may not want to admit them, the superior usually fears being dethroned by his subordinates. As I have indicated, all is not love between father and son. There is rivalry and hostility, too. The conflict between the young and the old was recognized in Greek tragedy and Biblical literature thousands of years ago. It finds expression in the business situation, too. The rivalry is usually more painful for the senior executive than for the subordinate, for the latter knows he has time on his side. Only rarely can the senior executive feel free to express his concern about the rivalry. More often he represses his fear. Its overt manifestation is his reluctance to develop others, lest they learn to do his job better than he and therefore replace him.

A senior manager is regarded by his associates as very capable and warm in his relationships with others. He has a young man reporting to him whom he regards as well qualified for advancement. But he will not delegate enough of the job to the younger man so that the latter can gain experience and management will have an opportunity to evaluate his performance. The manager repeatedly agrees to delegate more, but then "forgets." Finally, under pressure, he has delegated a part of his work, but continues to supervise it so closely that his subordinate has no feeling of responsibility. The responsible vice-president now has an acute problem: Either he will have to promote the subordinate without an opportunity to evaluate him, or he will run the risk of losing a good man.

Unless the executive who is doing the coaching and appraising can recognize that such feelings of rivalry, and their accompanying fears, are universal and not reprehensible, the coaching situation will be blocked with the effects of mixed feelings. If the existence of unconscious hostile feelings toward the rival is not brought out into the open with the superior by his own senior, and if the superior is not reassured by his senior that his position is secure, the underlying hostile feelings of the superior will come through in the relationship. In subtle ways, the superior will attack the subordinate, and the subordinate naturally will feel that he is being exploited rather than appraised. An executive must therefore be concerned with the effects of his behavior on the people below his subordinates and his own role as a subordinate as well.

It is not unusual for subordinates, recognizing this phenomenon to some degree, to discount the appraisal and forget about it as quickly as possible. Worse still, the subordinate may find his own ways to strike back at the superior, or he may, by displacement, take his anger out on his own subordinates. One of the most effective forms of rebellion is for the subordinate to decide that he does not want to be promoted further. No position frustrates higher management more than this one which, by rejecting what top management values very highly, also rejects identification.

Rear-guard action against the subordinate who rejects promotion may continue for a long time, but rarely does higher management realize that it may have had a part in frustrating ambition, impeding the full growth of a junior executive, and depriving the organization of a promising man.

5. *Relationship Unexamined.* As indicated earlier, much of psychological growth is the product of relationships, and

particularly relationships with identification figures. In a superior-subordinate relationship, both parties influence each other and both have a responsibility for the task. This is what is meant by the phrase "reporting to." In order to discharge his responsibility, each man must affect the other. Each has a different responsibility, but both share a joint task.

If they are to carry out the joint responsibility in the most effective way, they must be able to talk freely with each other. This dialogue cannot be limited to what the subordinate alone is doing. Each party must have a sense of modifying the other. The talks must also include the joint setting of goals and the opportunity to express how each feels about their working relationship. The question here is not of the adjustment of one to the other, but of the interaction between them. The former leads to passivity and conformity; the latter is a precondition for identification and growth. Specifically, the subordinate must be permitted to express his feelings about what the superior is doing in the relationship and what the subordinate would like him to do to further the accomplishment of the task.

No relationship is free of hostility. When the anger can be expressed in relatively controlled fashion, directed to furthering the task, it can serve constructive purposes. When it is suppressed, it creates more psychological friction in the relationship. But often the superior is reluctant to hear such feelings expressed. Sometimes he feels keenly about being the responsible executive, and therefore any such expression is disrespectful if not an outright personal attack. Often he is afraid that the anger of a subordinate is a reflection on his management or a threat to his position. Some superiors want to preserve the myth of "one big happy family," unable to recognize that there is no continuous state of happiness in any family.

Usually in a coaching situation, the relationship itself remains unexamined. The discussion centers around the performance of the subordinate alone in this case:

> Lee Brooks was promoted to a middle-management position as insurance supervisor on the basis of experience and background as well as recommendations from previous supervisors. Though he was qualified for the job, he was not outstandingly so. He wanted the position badly and the advancement potential which it opened for him. It was a plum for a man in his early thirties. Shortly after Brooks started his new work, his senior manager observed that he sometimes failed to finish assignments which he started and that he was lax in his supervision of those who reported to him. The senior manager held several discussions with Brooks, pointing out the need for improvement. Brooks agreed with the criticisms, promising to do better. But when no change occurred, the manager pressed him harder, pointing out that Brooks' future—his earnings, his family's well-being—depended on his improvement. He has increased his supervisory sessions with Brooks, but he has not yet asked himself or Brooks how he might be more helpful to Brooks. Nor has he looked at Brooks' job as something for which both of them share a responsibility.

When consideration is given only to the man's performance, there can be little change in some of the major underlying forces that affect performance. Furthermore, neither party is very comfortable because both are aware of what they are *not* talking about. The superior often has guilt feelings about appraising the subordinate. He is conscious of some of his own anger if the subordinate has not done too well; he is perhaps conscious of some of his rivalry and certainly of some of his own mistakes.

It is not surprising that the young executive is frequently insecure in his relationship with his superiors. Despite the first impression that may be conveyed, his own position is frequently "sink or swim." One mistake may obliterate a whole series of successes. It is not unusual that one of the more frequent complaints in business circles is, "I don't know where I stand."

Here is a situation in which management is trying to do its best to develop executives. Frequently it provides the finest possible facilities and outstanding instruction. Certainly no malice is intended. The problem is not that the intentions are bad or that no one really cares about what happens, but rather that few executives look carefully at the psychological significance of what is being done.

The result is often the opposite of management's intentions. For example, it is not unusual to find idealistic young executives who have become cynics. In management development programs, they have been encouraged to think of human needs and human relations, only to be mocked by the practices of their own superiors. Then there is the man who neatly compartmentalizes his paradoxical experiences. At one moment he espouses human relations principles and the next speaks of progress in his company as a dog-eat-dog proposition. Anger and disillusionment with the organization are not uncommon feelings, nor are psychosomatic reactions uncommon when other stresses are added.

This discussion yields a number of possible corrective steps:

1. If growth of executive capacity depends in a large measure on identification, and identification in turn depends

on the relationships between superior and subordinate, then the psychology of this sequence should be recognized by all executives who ought to be identification figures.

2. If the strength of the relationship between superior and subordinate is significantly related to the freedom each has to express his feelings to the other about that relationship, then the superior must enable the subordinate to express his feelings without being considered immature or inadequate. True, not everyone is skilled in eliciting feelings. There are, however, a good many seminars and sensitivity training laboratories where such skills can be learned.

3. If both superior and subordinate share responsibility for the subordinate's task, then coaching or development programs should be set up to provide means for appraising their joint efforts to fulfill this responsibility, and not only what the subordinate does alone.

4. If executives are to feel responsible for helping their subordinates to grow, two kinds of payment will be required. Each executive will need psychological payment in the form of similar attention from his own superior and he will also need to be compensated for development. One criterion by which an executive should be evaluated and paid is how well he helps others to grow, as shown by the records of advancement of his subordinates.

5. If the development of executives is important for the survival of the organization, then it is the responsibility of each executive to whom others report. It cannot be delegated.

Given the acceptance of this responsibility, a staff department devoted to management development can make an effective *complementary* contribution. The staff department can help the line executive develop his own coaching and interviewing skills. It can help him learn and apply understanding of individual and group psychology. It can keep him up to date on advances in business knowledge. In short, it can truly serve a development function. In such an arrangement, no longer would the staff be asked to solve huge, complex problems by training, with inadequate access to line executives and top management.

CHAPTER 17

Personality Clashes

ANOTHER ASPECT OF THE WORK SITUATION TO WHICH MANAGE-
ment gives considerable attention is the relationship of
subordinates with each other. Here, too, a closer look at the
problems of interrelationships may make coping with them
easier. These problems are often called "personality clash."
"Personality clash" is one of the most frequent reasons given
for discharging or transferring someone. Any argument
between two people could be called a personality clash.
When applied in administration, however, the term usually
refers to chronic conflicts.

It is as if the two people involved were charged with static
electricity. Sparks fly when they come near each other. When
they tire of argument, or try to avoid outbursts, they build
an insulation of cold formality around themselves. Then,
neither person can possibly hear what the other has to say,
and nothing the other person says can possibly be right.
Each has a rigid view of the other's purposes and position.
Any agreement between them is a truce; neither dares let
down his guard.

To you who must deal with such a clash in management, it

often seems that the parties are simply being obstinate. But the reason the problem is difficult for both the participants and those who want to help solve it is captured in the word "personality."

As has been shown, everyone has learned to cope with fears, anger, threats, and the like by establishing certain traits and favored ways of behaving. When you encounter someone else who needs to do things differently, your efforts to make him do it your way threaten his balance, while his refusal to comply threatens your balance. What seems to be rigidity is an effort at self-protection.

Efforts toward solution must be directed not at the clash itself but to relieving the underlying defensiveness.

DIFFERENT PERSONALITY STYLES

Perhaps the most common problem occurs when two people who must work together go at their job in quite different ways. One may be casual and the other meticulous. The first is driven to chronic irritation by the second. He cannot understand the concern for petty detail. He resents being nagged about crossing the t's and dotting the i's. The second man may view the first as lazy, careless, and unconcerned.

Neither is going to change his style no matter what the other man or the superior says. But if the attention of both can be directed to the results rather than the method, both can learn to accept the fact that each person is unique. Each therefore wants to work in the way that is most comfortable for him.

Five accountants worked together in an insurance company. Four of them had time to chat with each other. The fifth did not. Each had to do business with people from other departments. Four saw their people quickly and had time between appointments. The fifth never seemed to have extra time. To the four, the fifth was an eager beaver, trying to drive them as well as himself. To the fifth, the others did not want to do an honest day's work.

Their supervisor talked it out with them. He indicated what all were responsible for and how their performance was being judged. But, wisely, he added something else. He pointed out what they were *not* to do. This did two things: The four men now knew what they were supposed to do, including the limits set by their superior; the fifth man, driven by his superego to be overmeticulous and overconscientious, was in effect given permission not to be so conscientious. A pressure he could not take off himself was removed by the superior.

Where there is a simple difference in work style, it is often helpful to reaffirm the principle that the product is what counts and that each person is responsible to his superior for his performance, not to his co-workers. If two people with such varying techniques are working on a common task, the opportunity to talk it out with the superior is a step toward the possibility of tolerating each other.

TESTING THE LIMITS

One form of personality clash is that between superior and subordinate. Anyone who has children knows the experience called "testing the limits," one form of which is passive aggression, which was discussed in Chapter 10. The parent's words seem to mean nothing to the child. When, in desperation, father raises his voice, the child manages to do what he is supposed to.

Among adults, this experience is somewhat more refined. It is not unusual for subordinates to find various ways to vex the superior. Although the superior is likely to think that such provocations are entirely conscious and deliberately plotted, often they are not. Frequently they occur when people are too free and the boundaries are not clear. A person may in effect be asking his superior to take a stand so he can know to what extent he can depend on his superior for stable controls.

Moss Hart observed in his autobiography, *Act One*, that the only bad behavior he ever witnessed in the theater was "that ghastly moment when a star or a cast of actors became aware that their director was not in control of either the play or themselves. It is then that temperament sets in. . . ."[22] Mr. Hart suggested that temperament is a mask for panic that results when there is not a climate of security, and there is neither security nor peace when the director does not assume and maintain ironclad control of the play. Much the same could be said for a business situation.

This is not to say that democratic management is a failure. Rather, even democracy needs controls to prevent anarchy.

If people in an organization are not overcontrolled and oversupervised, then if a person is constantly demanding time and privileges and protesting that he is not being given enough freedoms, if he is apparently trying to provoke the superior's anger, it may be time to start making demands and requirements of him. The rules may have to be restated and expectations strongly reinforced. A firm, consistent attitude, far from threatening people who are testing the limits, gives them considerable comfort and lets them know the superior is indeed a superior. However, it should be clear that over-control can make these complaints legitimate.

INABILITY TO LET GO

Inability to let go is a crude way of characterizing an experience that occurs frequently in two kinds of situations. One involves continuing hostility between a man who is about to retire and the man he is supposed to be preparing to take his place. The second situation involves a man who has been promoted, but still has control over his former job, and the man who succeeds him.

Prospective retirement is, of course, fraught with many fears and anxieties. When a person is asked to train his successor, there is a finality to the prospect of retirement. It can no longer be avoided by trying to forget about it. A prominent executive who refused to choose and train a successor reflected the pain of the experience: "I can't stand having somebody like that around, knowing every time I look at him he's waiting for me to die."

A typical problem occurred with the head of a manufacturing department of a medium-sized company. He repeatedly postponed selecting and training a successor. When his superiors insisted he do so, and helped him find a suitable understudy, he gave the new man no work to do. The newcomer was soon complaining to others, aggravating the conflict.

A typical problem usually includes a typical mistake. The responsible vice-president dismissed the problem as a personality clash, leaving it to the two men to settle their differences. But they could not do so. The manufacturing head saw his assistant as a threatening rival whom he would not strengthen in any way. The assistant saw his boss as one who could not delegate any responsibility. The problem dragged on for six months and came to a head when the assistant offered his resignation.

At that point the vice-president intervened. When he began to understand the reasons underlying the conflict, he talked with the manufacturing head. He pointed out that although he could understand the man's feeling about retirement, the prospect was real and a successor would have to be trained. Together he and the manufacturing head spelled out what the new man would have to learn and the steps in which he would have to learn it. A timetable was arranged by which the manufacturing head would give up parts of his job. Once the reality of the situation was firmly defined, it became a factual starting point for both parties.

The manufacturing head still had his negative feelings, but his unrealistic method of coping with them had to yield to the responsibilities required of him.

The second situation is illustrated by what happened when the president of a subsidiary was made president of the parent company.

He was succeeded in the subsidiary post by a close friend. He could and did talk freely with his friend and they were readily able to resolve whatever differences arose. They saw each other socially and shared many experiences. Then the friend died, and a new man was appointed.

The senior president described his relationship to the subsidiary president as a personality clash. He said that, try as he would, he could not become friendly with the new man. He felt less and less in touch with the operation of the subsidiary. The subsidiary president seemed constantly to question the policies of his superior. Differences between the two became so unpleasant that both preferred to avoid a meeting.

Those who believe the job of an executive is to make quick decisions might well have fired the president of the subsidiary. Any successor, however, would have had the same experience.

The senior president presented his problem to a friend. Closer examination of the situation disclosed that he could not let go of the subsidiary he had once operated. He regretted that he was no longer as close to operations as he had once been. He tried to remain on intimate terms with operations through the subsidiary president. As long as a close friend headed the subsidiary, he could do so. But the new man needed freedom to operate his own organization. He needed the corporate president as a superior, not as a friend. He could not operate in the image of someone else. As long as his superior tried to make him into something he could not be, he was angry and resentful and the two were at odds. Once the superior heard himself say what he was really doing, he could see the situation in a different light.

RIVALRY

One of the more evident reasons for personality clashes is competitive rivalry. While rivalry is part of the process of growing up, both from childhood and through executive ranks, it cannot be permitted to become destructive to the organization. When the energy of the rivals seems to be directed more to the quarrel between them than to the tasks at hand, someone must help redirect their energies. He must also look at the way in which the work situation fosters destructive rivalry.

Rivalry is a perennial problem, which has its roots in the competition between children for the attention of the parents and between children and parents of the same sex. Situations that recapitulate early family experiences are natural settings for the occurrence of rivalry.

Often, managements unwittingly stimulate destructive rivalry between peers by putting people in unnecessarily competitive and therefore threatening situations. When, for example, a company president devotes most of his weekly staff meeting to comparing the cost cutting or profit performances of his vice-presidents, he is doing essentially what a parent does in comparing his children. To compare children unfavorably with each other in a taunting fashion is thinly disguised aggression. In this case, the president increases rivalry and resentment, and makes it more difficult for the vice-presidents to cooperate with one another. Furthermore, the greater the pressure he puts on them, the more likely he is to produce the same kind of squabbles that go on between children. Their response to his own aggression is displaced onto the rivals. This, then, seems to be personality clash.

If, instead, he were to direct his efforts to helping each vice-president do his job better, each would feel more supported and more worthy. Each would also feel less threatened by both the other vice-presidents and the president. In effect, the president would be using his aggression more constructively, directing it to problems rather than to people, and each of his subordinates could more easily do the same.

Failure to recognize this source of increased rivalry is

often extremely costly. It is not unusual to find various divisions of an organization spending more time and effort fighting each other and guarding themselves against each other than in forwarding the organization as a whole. In more than one company, the "enemy" is other departments, and this rivalry extends so far that departments conceal their promising young executives lest others try to steal them away.

SEVERE PERSONALITY PROBLEMS

An advertising manager had moved up rapidly in his company in just eight years. His behavior toward others in the organization was not pleasant, however. He viewed himself as superior to them and made no bones about telling them so. (The reader will recognize this as a hostility reaction.) He refused to have anything to do with his business associates off the job. His superiors were aware of his difficulties in getting along, but dismissed them because of his obvious talent. When he was promoted to a more responsible position, his behavior temporarily improved, and his job performance was excellent as long as he was working on immediate tasks.

But even the promotion began to pale, and he was soon criticizing his superiors. He submitted extended written questions to them about political and social problems that had nothing to do with his work. He assumed authority that was not delegated to him and demanded increasing time from his immediate superior. This behavior resulted in frequent arguments and, finally, a transfer. The company was still reluctant to lose his talents. But transfer rarely solves such problems. Soon his new boss was closing the office door to keep him out, and complaints began to come from other departments that he was intruding in their activities.

When the problem was discussed with him, the manager denied that he was creating any difficulty and felt that any differences with his superiors could be resolved by their joint discussion. In desperation, after repeated attempts to reach other solutions, his superiors finally let him go. They felt, however, that they had failed because they thought they should have been able to use his talents and resolve his difficulties.

This example highlights the fact that when a person has difficulties with almost everyone with whom he comes into contact, and these difficulties are chronic, his problem requires professional help. This man would be a difficult problem for a highly skilled therapist. No layman could reasonably expect to solve his problems.

From these examples, and the efforts made to resolve the problems, some simple suggestions seem worthy of consideration:

1. *Do not dismiss a conflict as "just a personality clash."* If people are in chronic disagreement, then an uncomfortable and possible destructive situation exists, not only for them but also for others, particularly subordinates. Such a situation may result from differences in personality style; from efforts to test the superior's control; because the superior cannot delegate; because of executive pressure that increases rivalry or severe personality disturbances.

2. *Do not procrastinate because the problem is unpleasant.* Do not expect it to solve itself. It rarely does. The opposite usually occurs. There is a tendency for the opponents to freeze in their attitudes and to marshal supporters and evidence for their point of view. Solutions require, first,

some way of breaking through these positions to get some of the respective feelings out in the open. The immediately responsible superior must be the third party who directs the antagonists away from each other and toward constructive solutions. He must also look at his own style of management as a possible stimulus to personality clashes.

3. *Ask yourself who is being threatened and why?* Can these threats be eased by an expression of the person's feelings about them, by reassurance, by firmness of support and direction? Or by changes in your mode of operation?

4. *Look at a changed situation to see if some need that one person was able to meet in his previous situation is now no longer being met.* Must he now sublimate his drives differently, less comfortably than before? Did he prefer to do what he was doing before? Has a support been taken away in the process of change? Can the person recognize this loss and be helped to find new supports? Can you make up for the losses he has experienced or provide the necessary support?

5. *Evaluate the extent of the conflict.* Has one person had difficulties for a long time and with many people? Is his problem chronic and repetitive? If so, the person is likely to require professional help. If several people or departments are involved, the clash is more likely to result from administrative pressure.

6. *If you are one of the parties to the clash, talk to a third party whom you can trust and whose judgment you value.* See how the problem looks when you express it aloud, and how it appears in the eyes of the other person.

7. *Finally, recognize that not all problems are soluble.* Some remain, unpleasant and unwelcome, despite our best efforts. Sometimes the only solution is to accept that fact and live with it.

CHAPTER 18

Management by Guilt

EVER SINCE THE PRE-WORLD WAR I DAYS OF INDUSTRIAL ENGI-
neering, many people have sought to make management a
highly defined process built around some basic assumption
about how that task can best be organized. We therefore
have such conceptions as management by task force, management by system, management by goals, management by
control, and management by coordination. In each of these,
the basic assumption is the primary determinant for organizing the executive's perception of his task. Each is a pur-
posive concept.

These structural efforts, which have been significant contributions to management efficiency over the years, are
intended to counteract behavior that might be irrational in
terms of the task to be done. They usually require a statement of goals and projected targets together with logically
deduced programmatic statements derived from these goals.
Organization charts describe who is responsible to whom for
what. Job descriptions tell in detail what the jobholder is
supposed to do. Appraisal systems provide for periodic eval-
uations of how the job is done. Personnel policies and pro-

267

cedures state the rules that govern employees from hiring to retirement.

This proposition assumes that people, for the most part, are rational. Therefore the more clear, specific, and comprehensive the organizational structure can be, presumably the more people will respond rationally within it. Generally speaking, these assumptions are valid. However, the *appeal* to rationality is frequently likely to be unsuccessful. Unless the effort to counteract irrationality also recognizes the sources of that irrationality and focuses attention on them, then it may be ineffective.

Sociologists have pointed out that in addition to the formal structure of an organization, there is an informal structure. The latter has more effect on the nature of its operations. Informal structure is created when formal structure fails to do its job. Formal structure often can be reorganized to include informal structure and thereby to adapt to organizational realities.

Much that passes for rational decision making, based on objective criteria, is also likely to be a product of a person's efforts to maintain his psychological equilibrium. Specifically, much of the irrational in management practices arises because of people's efforts to cope with their own anger and to avoid the anger of others. Executives go to great lengths to avoid conflict because of their discomfort with feelings of anger. But the very fact that they have angry feelings, when they often feel it is wrong to be angry, leaves them feeling guilty. With these two feelings to contend with, executives frequently make decisions in such a way that they can deny their anger to themselves and appease their superegos. In short, we speak of management by guilt.

The fact of anger and guilt as significant determinants of executive action goes unrecognized in management organizing, planning, and decision making. This problem, however, cannot be dealt with simply by changing organization structure.

GUILT-INDUCING PROBLEMS

FAILURE TO PRODUCE.

Here is a typical case, as reported by the executive who had to make the final decision about the man involved. Included are all the elements found repeatedly in management by guilt: disappointment in the man; failure to confront him realistically about his job behavior; procrastination in reaching a decision about him; cover-up compliments to ease the guilt of managerial anger; transfer to another position; finally, discharge.

Ewell Sturdy was in the new products division of a food products manufacturer. He was generally acknowledged in the company to be brilliant but lazy. He could develop information about a new market or a new field quickly, but he seemed unable to follow through to the point of action.

At the time of writing, he had been in the company more than fifteen years, the last year and a half in the same assignment. During his tenure in his present assignment, he had produced no innovations in product or market. As a result, he was not given a salary increase. Sturdy angrily protested, saying that he had rendered valuable service. In his view, he was being short-changed again by a company that had never fully recognized or utilized his talents. Though he had been complimented by superiors many times during his employment, he had never been adequately paid. He cited chapter and verse about his contributions. He attributed the company's failure to recognize him to the jealousy of his supervisors and political undercurrents in the company.

Sturdy thereupon talked with the comptroller, who was not his immediate superior. In addition to complaining to the comptroller about his own lot, he accused his superiors of criticizing the comptroller. When the comptroller investigated the alleged criticism, he found it to be wholly imaginary on Sturdy's part. This finding led the comptroller to talk with Sturdy's immediate superior, who investigated further.

The superior's investigation disclosed that Sturdy's past supervisors reaffirmed the present judgment that he was highly intelligent but never completed a job. None would have him back. Many said he should have been fired shortly after he was hired. They alluded to "high level influence" or his "family situation" as reasons for not doing so.

When Ewell's superior discussed these findings with him, Sturdy replied that he had indeed been moved many times, as a result of which he had had no opportunity to show what he really could do. Some of the areas to which he had been assigned were new and risky. Others had simply folded up. He quoted supervisor after supervisor, each of whom in one way or another had complimented him for good work or special accomplishment. A double check with the supervisors Sturdy had mentioned produced the same reply: They did not want him back.

Again the superior told Sturdy what he had found. Sturdy was at loss to explain the feelings of his former supervisors. Nevertheless, he still felt misjudged, poorly treated, and misunderstood. At first he wanted to prove himself anew to his present superior, but when he learned that he could have three months to find another job, he promptly set about looking for one.

But the story did not end with Sturdy's departure. The manager who had to discharge him was angry not only at Sturdy for failing to do his job, but also, more importantly, at his colleagues and superiors. The latter had passed the buck from year to year and thereby had allowed for denial and projection on Sturdy's part. With each transfer, they gave Sturdy a "Northeast promotion." They could not, of course, promote him. But they felt so guilty about their own anger toward him and their feeling that perhaps they, too, were at fault, that they compensated for their feelings with compliments and a "promotion." Not a real promotion, mind you; but an almost-promotion, a small raise and a fancier title.

Sturdy's superior felt he had been made the goat for everyone else's procrastination. He had to carry the responsibility—and the blame—for terminating a man of fifteen years' service.

Sturdy himself had been clearly victimized. Though his superiors repeatedly rationalized their behavior by saying they were trying to be fair, as a matter of fact their behavior was destructive. It was apparent early in his career with the company that he was not doing well. If, after a reasonable time, he had been terminated, he still would have been young enough to try other jobs in other companies. Conceivably, in one or another he might have found himself. As it turned out, he did not find himself, and worse still, he lost fifteen precious years. During all that time, he must have known he really was not doing well. He said he thought he had not been given adequate raises. Despite his accusations against others, he must have had some feeling that there was dissatisfaction with his performance. Yet when those who were dissatisfied covered over their dissatisfaction, he had no way of knowing his real situation. In effect, his superiors, out of their guilt feelings, killed his occupational chances with kindness. In the process, they hurt each other because each supervisor managed to transfer him to another. No doubt each felt guilty about unloading him on the other. They also hurt the company because the man drew his salary for years without producing.

The most sound, most effective behavior is based on reality. A person must have adequate reaction to his behavior if he is to govern it according to the realities he must deal with. Without adequate information about himself, he is operating in the psychological dark. When he discovers that he has had inadequate or incorrect information, usually after many years, he is then justified in saying that he has been treated unfairly. He has. Every man has a right to know in unmistakable terms how he is performing in his job. He is, after all, spending days and years of his life out of which he has a right to expect a reasonably satisfying return.

Such management by guilt is extremely costly to the organization in another way, as indicated by this conclusion that lay behind a recent arbitration award:

. . . In particular and notwithstanding the grievant's unhappy record, the arbitrator must take notice of the fact that the grievant was allowed to invest all of his working life with this (organization). This appears to have resulted from an overindulgent attitude on the part of those in charge and it must be regarded as condonation of the grievant's misconduct. It must be assumed that the long continued unrewarding policy of appeasement and of condonement to some degree must have lulled the grievant into a false sense of security and resulted in his periodic contemptuous attitude toward those in authority.

CONCERN FOR LONG-SERVICE EMPLOYEES

Often management by guilt arises out of misdirected concern for employees with long service. I do not mean to imply that long service should not be recognized and rewarded. I insist, however, that failure to tell them about their performance is a poor reward for such service.

An accountant was responsible for all phases of accounting, including projected costs of alternative decisions. He was in his mid-fifties, had spent thirty-five years with his company, the last fifteen as controller. He was not a college graduate, but had had specialized training. His many years in the business stood him in good stead. He was energetic, loyal, and noted among his superiors for running a well-disciplined department, but he rarely originated anything new.

In the ordinary course of events, his superior was replaced. His new superior, a vice-president faced with many other problems, left the controller pretty much to his own devices. They consulted on special occasions. As more and well-trained younger people entered the business, problems began to appear. People from other departments complained to the vice-president that the controller was intruding into their work. The controller complained that the company's standards were slipping. He was dissatisfied with prospective candidates for his job. He became increasingly critical of others and finally of the vice-president. He blamed his vice-president for not doing anything about the problems and the vice-president in charge of operations for causing them.

More and more vice-presidential conference time was devoted to the controller's problems. The controller, for his part, became more indiscreet in his complaints and more uncontrolled in meetings.

In a company reorganization, the controller's new superior turned out to be the much criticized vice-president of operations. The latter decided that it would be necessary to have a brutally frank discussion with the controller. The controller was shocked to be told straightforwardly about his behavior. He demanded to know why he had not been told by his previous superior, with specific examples of his behavior. Without such information, he had concluded that his performance was acceptable. In effect, he had been permitted to be irresponsible.

The confrontation brought about noticeable change. The controller's problems and behavior had been characteristic of him for a long time, so he was not going to be a new man. But he did have enough ego strength to be capable of making a conscious effort to improve his performance, and he did so. He could have done so long before.

An important function of the organizational structure in any business is to control impulsive behavior. The structure ideally facilitates productive behavior; ideally it also prohibits behavior destructive to the organization. The failure of the first vice-president to supervise pulled the structural rug from under the controller. He became increasingly uncontrolled in an almost desperate bid for controls. The cost over some years was: failure to train a successor; little initiative and innovation; impairment of team effort because of frictions with others; plus endless hours of vice-presidential worry and conference time.

OBLIGATION TO ANOTHER

A frequent problem that leads an executive to management by guilt is his anger toward someone to whom he feels obligated. He feels, therefore, quite consciously, that he has no right to be angry with the person who has been so loyal or helpful. He suppresses his disappointment and the anger that goes with it. He tries to find organizational solutions to his problems—new assignments, different tasks. These, however, never overcome his disappointment. Moreover, he continues to feel guilty for his hostility to his faithful subordinate. Inasmuch as he cannot express his anger directly, he unconsciously displaces his anger. It comes out in subtle critical ways and in assignments on which the target of his anger is bound to fail. Here is such an example:

A young executive took over the management of a small organization which had recently experienced a split among its owners. Two long-term, middle-management employees, Del and Mac, remained with the organization when the split occurred. They had a wealth of information about the company's operations. As a result, for several years both men were invaluable to the new executive. He felt further obligated to them because he was a relative of the family that owned the business and in effect they had been loyal to that family.

The senior of the two loyal employees, Del, was particularly helpful in orienting the new executive. The executive came to lean on him, seeing him as a knowledgeable and competent man in an elder statesman role. However, as time passed, it became apparent to the new executive that the company was not moving ahead as it should. The executive formulated plans for a larger and more profitable operation. He talked these over with Del. Despite his college education and his business experience, Del did not seem to understand what the executive had in mind. He protested about the likelihood of increased overhead and saw no need for additional management help. He seemed to learn nothing from attending trade association meetings or contacts with others in the same business.

Despite his lack of business imagination, Del was well liked. He spoke easily, met others freely, and impressed them. He was an excellent story teller and the life of any party he attended. He used these talents to help maintain employee loyalty. The executive, though recognizing that Del was no businessman, appreciated Del's support and tried to keep Del close to him, both in organizational structure and in personal contact. The executive was not altogether content with this arrangement, but he excused it by saying he enjoyed Del's company.

After a couple of years of putting up with what he perceived as Del's roadblock point of view, the executive discovered that the junior of the two loyal employees, Mac, was doing Del's thinking for him. Despite his loyalty to Del, the executive became angry enough to create a new assignment for Del, which was a combination of make-work and trivial duties. Del created further problems by talking too much about company business. Still, there was no open discussion of these problems. Instead, the executive, talking to others, would depreciate Del's family. Indirectly he was blaming Del for the alleged shortcomings of his children.

The executive continued to protest his loyalty to Del, saying that no one in the organization was more loyal to him or more dependable. This relationship continued for more than fourteen years, relatively unchanged. During this period, Del had many health problems. The executive believed them to be due to tension. He was unaware that he himself might have helped increase the tension, although he was painfully aware that somehow he had failed Del.

As the executive himself pointed out, Del was essentially a public relations man. He could have been, and in many ways was, highly successful at that job. But the executive, because of the operation of the mechanism of idealization, felt obligated to make something else of him, something he was not and could not be. When Del failed to meet these unrealistic expectations, after being pushed and prodded to greater heights, the executive saw him as an obstructionist. He punished him by putting him on the shelf and criticizing his family. For years Del lived with his boss' thinly veiled hostility and his feelings of failure. He paid a high psychological price, as did the executive, because the latter was guided by his guilt feelings instead of rational judgment.

A similar situation often occurs with spinster secretaries who in effect have married the business and who have served a major executive during a good part of their careers. With age and increased loneliness, they tend to become more isolated, frustrated, and rejected. This experience, in turn, often leads them to be irritable, discourteous, and sometimes openly hostile to younger employees. Most of the time, executives are reluctant to confront such a woman with her behavior, particularly if she cried when they first tried to do so. Yet, unless the woman is aware of the results of her behavior, she has little reason for changing it. More important to her, if she cannot change when the effects of her behavior are reported to her, she may well need professional help. The executive's failure to confront her deprives her of the leverage to get help. One important way for a person to learn that she needs help is to realize that, despite her best efforts, she is not performing adquately on that job.

Of course confrontation is no panacea, and it does not replace the empty loneliness such people live with constantly. If you and others in the organization make special efforts to help relieve the loneliness, you can thereby diminish the intensity of the anger. Usually when others try to befriend the lonely person, they are helpless without his cooperation. Sometimes it takes confrontation to bring about that cooperation.

THE URGE TO REFORM

Many people outside of managerial ranks have a picture of management as harsh, autocratic, and exploitative—and some executives are. However, management more often is destructive to people by procrastination and overkindness in mistaken and inappropriate effort to make people better. This example is a clear demonstration:

When, after he had been in the company for several years, Ed Allen's supervisors appraised him, they described him as an incompetent office manager. According to his superiors, he was limited in his ability; he had a poor personality; he was unable to handle help; he was unwilling to suggest, adopt, or agree to new ideas. His thinking was muddled and his decisions were never definitive. After this evaluation had been arrived at, he was transferred to another smaller office, which he also managed. There, shortly after his arrival, he acquired a new manager.

Allen presented a challenge to the new manager, so much a challenge that the manager tried for ten years to "develop" him. First, the new manager tried praise and encouragement. Allen's reaction was, "It's about time my work was appreciated and my expertness was recognized." There was no improvement in his work.

Next the manager tried toughness. This disturbed Allen for a while and he tried a little harder. But then he apparently decided his manager was basically intolerant and he would just have to live with intolerance.

The manager tried group pressure. He reviewed policies and procedures with all his immediate subordinates together. Allen changed some of his forms and managed to cut down on some paper work, but his cost-cutting efforts were sporadic and desultory at best.

Allen and his manager then talked at length and repeatedly, particularly about Allen's staff. Allen complained that he had not had enough help and that the help he did have was not good enough. Despite help offered him through the addition of automated equipment and the reduction of reports, the size of Allen's staff remained constant.

When all this effort failed, when ten years had passed, and when there continued to be complaint from higher management, someone else took over Ed Allen's work, and Ed was given early retirement.

This company prided itself on its lenient attitude to employees with long service. The price of its lenience can only be imagined. How much rejection and hostility did Allen experience from his superiors? With how much anger did his subordinates have to live over the years? By what stretch of the imagination could Allen possibly experience his work life as successful when all he knew was failure? No one knew the answers to these questions. No one had ever asked Allen about his feelings.

The guilt feelings of the company management were reflected in the impulsive way they got rid of him. When they decided to terminate him, among themselves they set a termination date. Six months before that date, they notified him that he would be terminated, paid him for the next six months, and had a man ready to step into his job the moment he was informed what would happen to him. In one day he was notified, fired, and paid off.

THE YOUNG VS. THE OLD

The movement of a younger man into a position of authority over older men usually seems to result in conflicting feelings in both parties, as was noted in Chapter 12. The younger man's feelings usually include some feelings of guilt that he has vanquished his older competitors. It is hard for him not to feel that he has taken away from them an opportunity for them to move up, and they may privately agree. His pleasure with his success is often tempered by an underlying disquiet. His guilt feelings make it difficult for him to make rational decisions, for so many of his decisions are tinged with the effort to appease the older men—without success. He seems to be chagrined, too, that nobody warned him of these feelings and the problems they produce. One young president put it this way:

I am many years junior to the other executives in our organization who report to me. Unfortunately the fact of age differences is seldom faced and the difficulties between us are blamed on poor communications. Differences in values, objectives and energy levels are responsible for the lack of rapport. They accuse me of by-passing my older, more experienced associates for the younger, more compatible ones. This is just an excuse for their own incompetence or inability. They criticize me for impatience, aggressiveness and judgment. The last occurs whenever I make a decision without consulting them. But they are extremely cautious, they lack aggressiveness and their judgment is markedly conservative. Of course, this conflict confuses the subordinates of these executives and leads to some choosing of sides. Can some method be devised that recognizes the possibility of this conflict immediately on the appointment of a younger man to an important managerial position with older subordinates? Might it not be beneficial to have frank discussions with the parties involved about the possibility of such problems developing? Would a committee method of decision making give some relief to me in my relationship with them?

The guilt here is most evident in the new president's inability to take charge. He sees only differences in orientation and style of administration. He does not see that the older men will continue to hang back and fight him until they are certain he is stronger than they. He is unconsciously afraid to be stronger, and therefore unrealistically feels guilty because he had surpassed older men. He would rather turn to a committee, in effect abdicate leadership, in an effort to appease them and his superego.[24]

CONFLICT WITH DIRECTION OF POLICY

Probably the most painful situation involving management by guilt takes place when an executive feels that he is being forced to take action that he feels is unfair or unwarranted. Without an adequate basis in his own mind for taking the action, he seizes upon some minor incident, which he then magnifies out of proportion. His anger becomes equally exaggerated as he reacts to his own guilt. But when the subordinate mounts his own attack, the superior finds himself even more on the defensive because he cannot cope with both the subordinate's anger and his own guilt feelings simultaneously.

Rusk was the manager of local operations of a large manufacturing company. He was in this position about five months when two of the company's more prominent directors visited his location. They had no criticism of his management, but they had plenty to say about his lack of social grace. He served them too much liquor, they complained, and he picked up the check for drinks in a local bar when one of them was officially the host. Not that Rusk drank too much—just that he lacked some of the social amenities. In their view, therefore, he should not be the local manager. Taking his cue from the directors, the president began to voice the feelings to the vice-president who was Rusk's superior, that the vice-president should begin looking for a new manager.

The vice-president felt Rusk was honest and diligent. He did not try to hide bad news. He had reasonably good knowledge of his operations. He had recently completed a building program within his budget. He apparently had the cooperation of his subordinates. True, he tended to be a little slow making decisions, he was not particularly astute, and he used too many words. On the whole, however, he was doing well where he was.

The pressure mounted from above, but there seemed to be no adequate managerial reason to discharge the man. The personality factors seemed not to be that important to the vice-president. Yet there was no question that the pressure was almost a direct demand that Rusk be fired. The vice-president kept a constant alert for an obvious managerial failure to serve as a cause for dismissal, or for an obvious demonstration of managerial success to support his contention that Rusk could manage satisfactorily.

Unfortunately, Rusk provided an opening for criticism just at this time. Not only was his budget proposal late in getting to the vice-president, but also his requests seemed unusually high. The vice-president attacked sharply. He said he would not tolerate a late budget and the high requests could have been avoided by advance planning.

This provoked counterattack by Rusk. He pointed out that his subordinates were permitted to authorize certain expenditures, though he was not. Several of his subordinates were officers of subsidiary corporations, but he was not—a direct slap as he saw it. He had been promised stock options and a bonus, but neither had materialized. In short, he complained, higher management demonstrated no confidence in him.

The vice-president did not argue with Rusk. He knew that Rusk's complaints were valid, and furthermore, that Rusk's observation was also valid. Higher management did not have confidence in him. He told Rusk what he should have told him in the first place, but his own guilt feelings had not let him; namely, that regardless of why he did not have top management support, since he did not have it, he might just as well find another job because he could never be successful in this company.

AGGRESSION AS A PROBLEM OF PERSONALITY

In previous examples, guilt has arisen with respect to aggression stimulated in a specific managerial situation. As was seen in Parts I and II, some people have chronic difficulty with their aggressions. These people have problems managing others. Thus people who ordinarily are nonautocratic become autocratic and perfectionistic as supervisors when influenced by guilt. What is evident in these situations is the executive's inability to satisfy his own superego, despite his constant striving for perfection, nor is anyone else able to satisfy his standards. The results are devastating to the growth of subordinates, though often they maintain a high level of performance as long as the supervisor is in control. The problem tends to grow worse as the supervisor grows older and his capacities begin to decline. As he is less and less able to meet his ideal performance, he tends to become more irritable, angry, and depressed. Here is a case in point:

A high-level executive has been with his company thirty years. Off the job he is relaxed, congenial, and popular. He is dedicated to whatever he may be doing at the moment—from bridge to fishing. He does not drink, but he is tolerant of others' drinking. He is active in church and charitable affairs. He is solicitous of his friends and he is generally a soft touch in charity.

His many talents led to his rise in the company. Supervision, however, is not one of his talents, except with those who are as talented as he. He is impatient with the average. He is excessively dominant to the point of arrogance. He is a poor teacher because he has the answers and is too impatient for his group to work out the solutions. He has a timid group of subordinates. He does not have time to provide all the answers, so he pays close attention to those projects in which he has an interest at the expense of the others and of his responsibility in general. Promising young men have left the organization as a result of his inadequate supervision. Among them was a man of long experience who should have been his logical successor.

Repeated discussions about his overconscientiousness and overdedication have gotten nowhere. Nor have "Dutch uncle" talks about delegating, patience in teaching, or giving his subordinates a chance to make mistakes made any difference. Moreover, he is becoming more pessimistic and moody as competition increases and new products are developed which are outside of his experience.

This man's "moods" will increase to the point where his underlying depression is obvious and he will ultimately require treatment. As a matter of fact, he actually needs treatment now, but neither he nor his superior can accept that fact.

In this situation the managerial problem is that the guilt-ridden man is in a supervisory position. In the following case, the boss is unwilling to recognize that such a person, despite his obvious talents, cannot supervise:

A fifty-year-old man has fifteen years of experience in the business. He is intelligent, well educated, and imaginative. He is pleasant, courteous, extremely considerate of others and has a high sense of ethics. He is a good salesman. His physical appearance impresses others. He is essentially a very wholesome and somewhat naive individual. He is extremely anxious to avoid hurting another person's feelings, and has a great distaste for any unpleasantness in his relationships with other people. He is very trusting of people. He is somewhat indecisive and tends to look at a person's virtues rather than his performance.

His boss asks, "How can this man be made an effective manager over 150 people and get results? His leadership tends to waiver and his indirect approach leaves people not fully recognizing the problem or what he wants to accomplish.

"How can this man be helped to become effective within the framework of his own personality? He obviously has the capacity to do the job, but the effective leadership of the organization appears to be lacking. His reliance on gentle persuasion is insufficient."

This man's superego will not let him tolerate his own aggressive feelings or the hostility of others. He contains his own feelings and denies the anger of others. Short of extended treatment (unlikely at his age and because he does not regard himself as being maladjusted or sick) he cannot change his superego. His boss would do both himself and the man a service by not making him a supervisor.

A more subtle and therefore more difficult situation involves the executive who in repeated small ways puts himself in a bad light. His errors in judgment are not in themselves significant; that they occur, however, raises doubts about his judgment in the eyes of his superiors. He leads when he should wait for support, and he waits for support when he should lead. Throughout all this, he is the picture of agreeableness. Apparently he hears the criticisms of his performance, but his behavior does not change. His superiors become angry with him, and then disappointed. Then some trivial event occurs, and they fire him. "Not qualified for higher responsibilities," they say. The man himself is dismayed. "But they never told me they were dissatisfied," he says. "I asked them to tell me why, but they can't. I did a good job. It must be strictly political."

The executive is partly right. His superiors cannot cite chapter and verse. When they try, the reasons are so trivial that they cannot specify the reasons to themselves. They just do not know, and though they are uneasy for not knowing, they are certain they have made the right decision. Each trivial incident has aroused their anger. But it is not appropriate to have much anger for trivial incidents, so the anger is repressed. The executive is such a fine fellow and works so hard that his bosses feel guilty for the momentary anger. Guilt increases as each incident provokes more anger and more repression. Finally they build up enough residual anger, enough guilt for feeling angry, and then more anger for feeling guilty, that they strike out against their subtle tormentor, even to the point of feeling like fools because they do not have a significant objective reason for firing him.

Though neither the executive nor his superiors nor others familiar with the situation can understand what happened, a second careful look usually tells the story. Much of the time, what appears to be precipitous and unwarranted firing results from those guilt feelings in a person that motivate him to seek punishment and rejection from others. In other words, he manages to put his worst foot forward and to be punished by being fired, to assuage his own guilt feelings. At the height of success, he manages to defeat himself, but is never able to see the seeds of his defeat in his own behavior. This is the unrecognized pattern: guilt; self-punishment by provoking others; guilt in others for having aggressive feelings toward him; build up of aggression and guilt; impulsive firing, to be relieved of the guilt and the provocation to aggression.

A SECOND LOOK

These examples are only a few of the instances in which anger and guilt for anger become significant determinants of executive action. According to the theoretical considerations in Part I, these behaviors occur when the aggressive drive is stimulated beyond the ego's capacity to deal with it more constructively, and the superego reacts to the rising aggression.

Many times it is difficult to recognize subtle forms of your own anger or that of others. Often you have fairly evident cues in your own behavior: a feeling of uneasiness and self-criticism after a decision about another person; feeling less comfortable with the other person than before; avoiding the other person, seeing him less, having difficulty conversing with him; criticizing him more to others repeatedly or justifying your own actions repeatedly; giving him the dirty jobs; or bending over backwards to be nice to him, as if he were something special.

As you review problem situations with this idea in mind, you should ask yourself what were the conditions under which your own or someone else's anger and guilt might have been stimulated. They may include one or more of these:

1. Real or imagined attack by someone else
2. Threat to self-esteem, violating the ego ideal, values, or rules of living
3. Feeling of being manipulated, overcontrolled, exploited or imposed upon, or otherwise made to feel inadequate
4. Feeling of being disappointed or let down, reflecting the frustration of dependency needs, expectations or support
5. Lack of clear structure, making it difficult to know what one is supposed to do and not do
6. Stimulation of rivalry with someone else, whether subordinate, colleague, or superior
7. Failure to provide adequate controls for people who need structure to help them control their anger

If you recognize that you or someone else is angry and that you are trying to avoid saying so, then the sooner you can put an end to the game of make-believe, the better for both parties. This does not mean open warfare or a verbal slugging match. Rather, it requires that, recognizing your anger, you control it sufficiently to sit down with the other person and state the problem, together with your feelings about it. Then you have the often difficult task of hearing the other person out. This is where the guides to listening (Chapter 15) are particularly important.

What was particularly threatening to the other man? What made him so afraid (often unconsciously) that he had to defend himself in this way? You cannot ask him these questions, nor could he give you adequate answers if he wanted to, but you can sense some of the feelings the subordinate might have had in the situation. Your awareness of such feelings, however vaguely he understands them, will help him gain another perspective.

If the problem has to do with job performance, it is important to reassess whether he can do what is expected of him. Too often people are expected to make drastic changes in their personalities, which is impossible. Are you asking too much? What kind of help will he, with his particular assets and shortcomings, need to get the job done? Here it might be helpful to review the personality types discussed in Part II.

In fact, does he belong in this organization? Regardless of whether he has not been able to grow, or should not have been hired in the first place, or does not fit with the new management, or some other reason, is this really for him? If the man really does not have a reasonable opportunity to satisfy himself and the organization, then he might be better off in another organization where he can savor success. It is a fairly common experience that many men were boosted along in their careers by being fired, an action that required them to find some more rewarding work.

This is not be used as a rationalization for wielding the axe of discharge. Irresponsible treatment of human beings is nothing less than sadistic behavior, which no rationalization will ever justify.

A more responsible way of facing this problem is to spell out the pros and cons and weigh the alternatives. A clear statement of fact as you see it is an important part of his reality. You may not be completely right, but you must act on your own judgment, and that in itself is fact for the other person.

If you and the subordinate together decide the subordinate must go, or if you decide it yourself (assuming that the man is not being fired for cause), then you can give him invaluable help finding another job. Probably you know companies other than your own, and one may well have a place where the subordinate can make a contribution. You do not have to pass him off on someone else. You have only the reasonable responsibility for reporting his abilities and the conditions under which they thrive. If you can also indicate the conditions under which the subordinate does not do well, your honesty will command the respect of the other organization and make it more willing to employ the subordinate. Some executives do this themselves, some use their personnel departments, and some use the same executive recruitment agencies that are finding a replacement to place the man who is departing. Whatever is done along these lines, you will feel that you have done your best by the subordinate, and the latter will probably feel that he was treated fairly and with consideration for his dignity as a human being.

A fundamental guideline in this, as in any other human relations situation, is the question, "What are the equities in this situation?" What is fair to the man and to the organization? Decision by equity is a high sounding phrase. It is not easy to define. It neither punishes the man nor overcompensates him. Punishment is thinly disguised anger. Overcompensation results from not too thinly disguised guilt. Either behavior leaves both parties feeling angry, for when one "bends over backwards," he leaves the other person with the feeling that he does so to make up for a wrong or that he is patronizing the other.

Epilogue

WE HAVE SPOKEN MUCH ABOUT OTHERS—THIS CASE, THAT EX-
ample, a further problem. Between the lines you will have
seen an occasional fleeting but sharp reflection of yourself.

If you are like most people, however, you will see more
of those aspects of your personality that you dislike than
those which you value. That is, you judge yourself more
harshly than others do. As a result, you are likely to underestimate your impact on your subordinates and colleagues.
And you are also likely to underestimate the value of your
relationship with them when they are under emotional stress.
You may therefore feel reluctant to try to help. You may
even feel unable to change whatever forces in your own
organization contribute to stress. These are natural feelings
for which you need not apologize. But neither should you
fail to realize that even small efforts on your part can make
a significant difference to the well being of others.

Despite your best efforts, you will sometimes make mistakes, and some of your mistakes may cause stress for others.
But being an executive who carries on a continuing relationship with your subordinates, again and again you will have

an opportunity to remedy your mistakes and to be an agent of strength.

To accept the importance of your own humanness in the lives of others is to understand an important meaning of your own life.

References

1. MONTAGU, M. F. ASHLEY, *Prenatal Influence*. Springfield, Ill.: Charles C Thomas, 1962.
2. LIEBERMAN, MICHAEL W., "Early Developmental Stress and Later Behavior," *Science*, 141:824–825, August 30, 1963.
3. HINKLE, LAWRENCE E., PLUMMER, NORMAN, and WHITNEY, L. HOLLAND, "The Continuity of Patterns of Illness and the Prediction of Future Health," *Abstracts, Thirteenth International Congress on Occupational Health*, 1960.
4. DUNN, JAMES P., and COBB, SIDNEY, "Frequency of Peptic Ulcer among Executives," *Journal of Occupational Medicine*, 4:7, 343–348, July 1962.
5. CARON, HERBERT S., WARDWELL, WALTER I., and BAHNSON, CLAUS B., "Stress and Coronary Disease: The Responsibility Hypothesis." Presented to the American Psychological Association 1963 Annual Meeting.
6. PELL, SYDNEY, and D'ALONZO, C. ANTHONY, "Acute Myocardial Infarction in a Large Industrial Population," *Journal of the American Medical Association*, 185:11, 831–838, September 14, 1963.
7. LEVINSON, HARRY, "Alcoholism in Industry," *Menninger Quarterly*, XI:4, Supplement, 1957.

8. TRICE, HARRISON M., *Alcoholism in Industry.* New York: The Christopher D. Smithers Foundation, 1963.
9. ERIKSON, ERIK H., "Identity and the Life Cycle," *Psychological Issues,* 1:1, 1959.
10. CABOT, LOUIS, "Ethical Responsibilities of Business," *Stanford Graduate School of Business Bulletin,* 31:3, 70–76, 1962.
11. BAUMHART, RAYMOND C., "How Ethical Are Businessmen?" *Harvard Business Review,* 39:4, 6–7 ff., July-August 1961.
12. FLEISCHMAN, EDWIN A., "A Study of the Leadership Role of the Foreman in an Industrial Situation," Personnel Research Board, The Ohio State University, Columbus, Ohio, 1951.
13. DRUCKER, PETER F., *The Practice of Management.* New York: Harper & Row, 1954.
14. LIKERT, RENSIS, *New Patterns of Management.* New York: McGraw-Hill Book Co., Inc., 1961.
15. MCGREGOR, DOUGLAS, *The Human Side of Enterprise.* New York: McGraw-Hill Book Co., Inc., 1960.
16. RANDALL, CLARENCE, "Business, Too, Has Its Ivory Towers," *New York Times Magazine,* July 8, 1962, pp. 5 ff.
17. WATSON, THOMAS J., *A Business and Its Beliefs.* New York: McGraw-Hill Book Co., Inc., 1963.
18. SCHEIN, EDGAR H., "Management Development as a Process of Influence," *Industrial Management Review,* May 1961, pp. 59–77.
19. MCGREGOR, *op. cit.,* pp. 77–89.
20. GUEST, ROBERT, *Organization Change: The Effect of Successful Leadership.* Homewood, Ill.: Irwin Dorsey, Inc., 1962.
21. LIKERT, RENSIS, "Motivational Approach to Management Development," *Harvard Business Review,* 37:4, 75–82, July–August 1959.
22. HART, MOSS, *Act One.* New York: Random House, 1959.
23. SCHEIBER, ISRAEL B., "Arbitrator's Opinion and Interim Award in the Case of Schema Kaufman," American Arbitration Association, February 8, 1963.
24. ZALESNIK, ABRAHAM, "The Human Dilemmas of Leadership," *Harvard Business Review,* 41:4, 49–55, July–August 1963.

Index